HEALTH ON DEMAND

Praise for

HEALTH ON DEMAND

"An empowering and compelling book that should be read by everyone. It is simply that good."

– David M. Lawrence MD, former Chairman and

CEO, Kaiser Foundation Health Plan and Hospitals, Inc.

"Healthcare is personal. Dr. Subramani has created a powerful and engaging platform to help you identify, rectify and achieve your version of health success."

– Paul Spiegelman

New York Times best-selling author of *Patients Come Second*

"Dr. Subramani offers insight into how medicine and technology will transform how healthcare is delivered and consumed. He is an advocate for patients truly becoming co-pilots in their care. A better and smarter patient will revolutionize the future of medicine."

– Franklin Cockerill MD

CEO, Analyte Health; Past CEO,
Mayo Medical Laboratories and Emeritus Professor and Chair,
Department of Laboratory Medicine and Pathology, Mayo Clinic

"An excellent resource for patients, doctors and everyone who wants practical solutions to improve our healthcare system. This book is highly accessible, based on solid research that can and will make a difference. If you are interested in changing your healthcare, then read this book."

– Amy Duross
Executive Director, GE Ventures, Incubations

"*Health On Demand* is a well-researched, clearly organized, comprehensive road map to a better you... the smart health consumer."

– David Davidovic

Founder PathForward; former VP and Global Head, Commercial Services Roche & Genentech

"Dr. Subramani outlines the digital disruption that must be led by consumer revolution! Smart patients will push the many stakeholders to change current practices, behaviors and incentives—a change that will be needed to transform our health system."

– Ramin Bastani

CEO, Healthvana

"This is one book that has a complete and clear path about the future of our nation's healthcare. It should be read by patients, doctors, insurers, digital innovators—basically anyone looking to better their health, lower costs and become part of a digital health revolution."

– Sridhar Murthy

Digital Health Investor, Past CEO, Analyte Health

"Whether you want to learn more about how innovative companies are changing how we consume health or you're trying to find faster, smarter, better, cheaper ways to access healthcare, *Health On Demand* is your roadmap."

– Daniel Burrus

New York Times best-selling author of *Flash Foresight*

"Dr. Subramani's passion and enthusiasm for all the possibilities occurring in the healthcare space is riveting."

– Henry Albrecht

CEO and Founder, Limeade

"If you are serious about your health, whether you are using an app or device to track your health and wellness success, the contents of this book will practically guarantee your ability to get faster, better, smarter and cheaper healthcare."

– Michael Heinrich

CEO, Oh My Green

HEALTH
ON DEMAND

Insider Tips to Prevent Illness
and Optimize Your Care
in the Digital Age of Medicine

Ramesh Subramani MD, MBA, MPH

New York

HEALTH ON DEMAND

Insider Tips to Prevent Illness and Optimize Your Care in the Digital Age of Medicine

Published in New York, New York, by Morgan James Publishing. Morgan James and The Entrepreneurial Publisher are trademarks of Morgan James, LLC.
www.MorganJamesPublishing.com

The Morgan James Speakers Group can bring authors to your live event. For more information or to book an event visit The Morgan James Speakers Group at www.TheMorganJamesSpeakersGroup.com.

Shelfie

A **free** eBook edition is available
with the purchase of this print book.

CLEARLY PRINT YOUR NAME ABOVE IN UPPER CASE

Instructions to claim your free eBook edition:
1. Download the Shelfie app for Android or iOS
2. Write your name in **UPPER CASE** above
3. Use the Shelfie app to submit a photo
4. Download your eBook to any device

ISBN 978-1-63047-676-2 paperback
ISBN 978-1-63047-677-9 eBook
ISBN 978-1-63047-678-6 hardcover jacket
Library of Congress Control Number:
2015909594

Cover Design by:
Chris Treccani
www.3dogdesign.net

In an effort to support local communities and raise awareness and funds, Morgan James Publishing donates a percentage of all book sales for the life of each book to Habitat for Humanity Peninsula and Greater Williamsburg.

Get involved today, visit
www.MorganJamesBuilds.com

Habitat
for Humanity®
Peninsula and
Greater Williamsburg
Building Partner

Dedication

To you and to all patients...please start the revolution!

Thank You!

To my family, friends, colleagues, and
my beautiful wife Sanjivini,
for their tireless support of this book

CONTENTS

FOREWORD   xi

PROLOGUE   xiv

INTRODUCTION   xviii

Section I: Digital Revolution   **1**

1   CEO Of Your Health   3

2   Prescription For Change   11

3   Your Digital Game Plan   22

Section II: Digital Prevention   **31**

4   Find A Digitally Savvy Doctor   33

5   An App A Day…Keeps Your Doctor Away   39

6   Your Blood Can Predict Your Future   52

7   Train With Doctor Google   65

8   Add An Alarm System To Your Body   74

9   Upgrade Your Brain   85

10   "Google Map" Your DNA   90

11   In The End, You Can Fix Yourself   97

12   Make Public Health Your Digital Ally   103

Section III: Digital Optimization   111

13 The Need For Speed   113

14 The Price Is Right (Or At Least Transparent)   129

15 Use The Doctor In Your Pocket   135

16 Plug Into Patient Networks   143

17 Seek Tailored Treatments   149

18 The Doctor Will See Your Cells Now   156

19 Care Gets A Makeover   162

20 Siri, What Did My Doctor Say?   168

21 Complement Your Care   173

22 Care Takes Flight   181

23 Connected Doctors Heal the System   186

24 Digital Health In Action   191

CONCLUSION   211

ABOUT THE AUTHOR   215

APPENDIX A LIST OF COMPANIES   217
AND STARTUPS

APPENDIX B ADDITIONAL RESOURCES   228

ENDNOTES   229

FOREWORD

We are at a "grand inflection" in the evolution of healthcare delivery and individual engagement. I am mainly an active observer, but I observe from the perch of having been in the middle of medical education and practice, state and national policy, innovation and technology—as a transplant surgeon, former US Senator, and healthcare entrepreneur.

When I speak with healthcare leaders, fundamental challenges continue to come to light. The most compelling and persistent of these is the pressing need to engage patients in their own care. "Value-based care" may have started as a buzzword, but it is becoming our future.

Containing healthcare costs has appropriately become the leading edge of healthcare reform, but quality must remain central to care. The focus on quality cannot be the personal crusade of the provider alone; individuals and patients, I truly believe, will soon drive the market to the cost-quality balance.

Health On Demand is a step in that direction. This book empowers and engages patient-consumers by sharing practical and accessible tools for taking control of their own health. It explains the necessity and value of knowing your own health options and introduces myriad new tools to do so. It is both a road map and a call to action—for the patient-consumer and for healthcare providers.

The Affordable Care Act hopes to entice young, tech-savvy health consumers to enter the marketplace. With the high deductibles inherent in the ACA, this next generation of patients will face a different healthcare landscape than their parents navigated. They need a different solution: a partnership.

Partnership means transparency—not just in some aspects, but in everything: quality, cost, and outcomes. Legislation alone will never be enough to achieve that type of transparency. The power to demand true transparency is in the hands of the newly empowered patient and comes from taking charge of one's own healthcare and expecting excellence from the system.

How do we do that? We prioritize our own healthcare education. We avail ourselves of the most progressive technological options. We acknowledge that the status quo is not acceptable and we continue to demand excellence knowing the path forward is paved with change. We invest in building a system that will serve not just ourselves, but our children's and our nation's future.

But while change takes work, Dr. Subramani understands that navigating the healthcare system can be daunting. Though we all have some responsibility, none of us carries the full responsibility. *Health On Demand* is Dr. Subramani's prescription for change directed to both individual patients and the healthcare ecosystem at large, empowering to both.

Every day we make choices about our lives, and no longer are choices about our healthcare out of our hands. The future of healthcare in America depends on the rise of the patient-consumer and making the most of this historic opportunity. On behalf of Dr. Subramani, I invite you to learn and to change.

Senator William H. Frist, MD

PROLOGUE

How We Got Here

Medicine over the past 50 years has gone through a grand and brilliant evolution; now humans live almost twice as long as they did just a hundred years ago. But we also live in a time of limited access, high costs, and confusing inefficient processes. This is my take on the key issues that have brought us here.

In short, the *demand for healthcare is outpacing our capacity and resources*. One reason for this is that our 80 million Baby Boomers are entering their high health-consumption period. We don't have enough doctors, nurses, physician assistants, nurse practitioners, or field health workers to meet demands. In the U.S., there is an estimated shortage of 100,000-200,000 physicians.[1] As a result, doctors are seeing 40 patients a day in many clinics, which, shockingly, equates to about seven minutes spent with each patient.

Another reason demand is outpacing resources is that life expectancy has gone up by 12 years over the last 20 years. People continue to live longer despite complex medical conditions such as heart attacks, strokes, and infections—conditions that were automatically fatal in the past. By 2050, there will be over one million people living past the age of 100 in the world![2] This is good news, but unfortunately, longevity comes with a hefty medical price tag.

Our investments in medical research actually worked

Diseases that were life-ending just two decades ago can now be survived thanks to technological advancements. For example, heart transplants and Left Ventricular Assist Devices (LVADs)—a mechanical pump that is surgically attached to a heart—are each good examples of how technology can extend lives. Up until 10 years ago, LVAD didn't exist for individuals with failing hearts. In this way advanced **medical technology is contributing to an older, more complicated population**.

We have an "intellectually bottlenecked" system

In short, medical knowledge and know-how are—for the most part—the sole province of doctors. This is how it's been for the last 200 years. In that time, patients have become trained to "**go see the doctor**" whenever they need an annual exam, have a sore throat, injure their shoulder, or experience other minor illnesses. They have been **trained to let the doctor take the lead** in determining which medical tests they should get, which specialists they should see, and what types of follow-up appointments they should make. The underlying assumption has remained the same: the average patient does not have the intelligence to digest medical information, or interest in being the "driver" of their own care. The dynamic is **very one-sided and this asymmetry needs to change**.

We are over-dependent on doctors

Having the doctor do it all is one of the biggest cost drivers. Consider that it costs about $1 million to attend medical school and go through residency training. Many of the tasks a doctor performs can be done more economically by a mid-level provider (e.g., nurse practitioner), or through technology that is connected to less costly training. Given the shortage of doctors today and the exorbitant cost of training a single doctor, this is absolutely the wrong model. It will not deliver the care we need, or deserve, at a price we can afford. This theme is also called "right sizing" care.

Our "system architecture" is not responsive to innovation

Exploding medical science and options make it impossible (and impractical) for a single physician to "know it all." So, more so than ever before, general practitioners and family physicians must rely on their specialists and refer patients out in order to assess, diagnose, and address many medical problems. But there is also a huge deficit of specialists in many medical fields, especially in rural areas, creating additional inefficiencies and bottlenecks. Moreover, this current model of **"encounter-driven medicine"** is also outdated and inefficient. Patients are not "encounters." Yet this is the way the system sees them.

Healthcare's biggest Achilles heel is communication and coordination

Healthcare, by all parties, is notorious for **poor or non-existent communication** practices. People may not share their worries or health concerns with their families. Rushed by a seven-minute visit, patients withhold information from their doctors. Doctors have varying degrees of patient communication skills. Patients are afraid of asking their doctors important or embarrassing questions.

Patients often forget what their doctor tells them. These issues keep people from engaging—**they stay on the sidelines in many cases and may think, why bother?**

Absent of significant changes, our current infrastructure will not be able to keep pace with the complexity and demands that will be placed upon it. Given its importance, we cover communication in later chapters in more detail.

INTRODUCTION

I wrote this book for my patients, friends, and colleagues. It collects my observations and experiences across emergency medicine, venture investing, strategy consulting, and health entrepreneurship. Over this time, I had the opportunity to invest in revolutionary innovation and work with the broad ecosystem that is the engine of our system: namely for insurers, pharma, health systems, diagnostics, & medical device companies. Most recently I serve as Chief Medical Officer for a leading digital health company that has transformed the patient experience by lowering costs and improving access and quality.

This journey transformed my view of how to help patients and improve our health system. It is from these combined experiences, and from seeing everyday people in the ER, that I hope to make this insider view relevant for you.

The **digital health revolution** has offered a singularly unique time in our history where all people can truly **become engaged**

in their own health. In fact, I outline and discuss how over 250 companies and technologies are transforming the health industry landscape. This notion that patients (like you) can finally take better control of their health destiny is how this book was born. The digital health promise is faster, better, smarter, and lower cost care that will help you to stay healthy, pre-empt disease, and receive optimized care.

Patients are confused about their care options. They don't know how to access care in an effective way. They are tired of being nagged about their eating or exercise habits. They are worried about their increased cost burden. They are worried about healthcare reform, but they don't really know much about it. They are unsure about how to communicate about health concerns and needs. By empowering patients, this book aims to fix these problems.

To define digital health from a patient-centric view, I would say it is the combination of the **hardware** (devices, sensors, platforms, diagnostic tools) and **software** (apps, websites, algorithms) that together create solutions that enable patients to become more active co-pilots in **diagnosing conditions and receiving care more efficiently.**

Even though I have been in healthcare for almost two decades, ironically, I personally am in search for a better health experience. So in many ways this book is for me and for my fellow physician and nurse colleagues. I hope they use it to help their patients and themselves.

In fact, I find that most doctors don't know what is contained in these pages. They're busy keeping their practices going: dealing with the ever-increasing patient loads & the huge amount of often conflicting scientific information being thrown at them. Most were trained in the medical practices of the 1970s, '80s, and '90s—long before the remarkable technological changes that were brought on by the Internet and other advancements. So don't expect your doctor to be up-to-date with all these innovations. In this sense, *you may have to coach your doctor.*

So this book is for you, them, and me. We are all health consumers in the end.

In contrast to books about fixing the system, this book is also about *changing the game.* And empowering patients is the only way this "game" will truly change! With $2 trillion of health expenses providing "life support" for the current system, **all stakeholders need to focus on patient empowerment.** This concerted focus is the only way the system can change course. For those of you who are wondering, we have already lost—the current system won't get us to where we need to be.

This book, however, will not attempt a detailed discussion of how expensive healthcare is. Too many other books have already covered that topic. The current focus of the system is that we need to control costs. But singularly focusing on and struggling to control costs in a broken system doesn't fully make sense. We now have **options to actually change the system.**

That said, I don't want to make light of the complex organization needed to deliver healthcare. We want smart and incentivized doctors, safe and effective medications, technologies that will keep us well, and hospitals that focus on healing and providing outstanding care.

There are real improvements and notable trends happening:

- Patient safety initiatives; preventing errors like wrong medication or surgeries on the wrong limb

- Navigation & coordination efforts for better patient experience and more efficient flow through hospitals and clinics

- Reducing hospital purchasing costs and waste

- Improving clinical trial efficiencies so that drugs can be developed faster

These are some of the innovations, I believe, that will dramatically improve our current system. I applaud all the scientists, doctors, nurses, hospital workers, innovators, technologists, and all the stakeholders who work tirelessly to improve healthcare.

But in the end, to save healthcare, we need a *consumer revolution!* In fact, what you do as an engaged consumer may likely be more important than what your doctor does toward ultimately having a long and healthy life. Don't expect the change we need to only come from the current system; it has too many conflicted dependencies and is ultra-focused on high utilizers of care. Because of all of these issues the current system is too clogged to truly get us to the transformed health experience that we deserve.

From my vantage point as an emergency physician-turned-strategy consultant, venture capitalist, and now entrepreneur, I see digital technology enabling the development of 4 major changes in the *delivery* of healthcare. Let me briefly sketch them here. In short, medical care, with your help, will become:

1. *Faster* – in diagnosis, treatment, and outcome realization; less centralized, **more distributed** and available on demand in bite-size units of care.

2. *Better* – more **predictive and pre-emptive,** rather than, reactive care.

3. *Smarter* – meaning treatments customized to your genes, cells, culture, gender, and ethnicity. This initiative is also known as **precision medicine.**

4. *Cheaper* – providing **more value** for your healthcare dollar and better utilization of resources.

You Are The Solution

I strongly believe that **Smart Patients** (you) can actually "save" our healthcare system. Demand the system to produce more innovation, convenience, and quality—and in doing so achieve a lower cost for health delivery. Since every one of us will become a patient one day, this means all of us are leading this change.

What are the characteristics of a Smart Patient? They…

1. **Are connected directly** with all the new ways to become empowered (engaging in online resources, digital health offerings, etc.).

2. **Understand the kind of innovations** that will likely make the biggest difference for their own or their family's health.

3. **Know how to engage** with the different facets of the system such as accessing the right care at the right time. They are also better equipped to receive the care that is delivered.

4. **Demand the right set of changes** that will transform the model from one that is dependent on physicians to one that enables patients to be active co-pilots.

Smart Patients will be able to drive down the overall cost of care. According to Dr. Michael Roizen, 70% of US medical costs and about $1.3 trillion worth of related costs stem from problems that are amenable to health education and coaching.[3] In short, Smart Patients will cost healthcare less.

What's The Catch?

Asking the patient to take charge and *take responsibility* is a *revolutionary change*, one that will forever alter the dynamics of the patient-doctor relationship. The answers to the questions "What does it mean to get healthcare?" and "Whose responsibility is it to keep the patient healthy?" are changing. It's becoming the patient's responsibility to maintain good health. Because patients will have so many more choices than ever before, they'll have to learn how to discriminate between options so they get the right care, at the right time, and at the right price.

So Why Read This Book?

In addition to providing a framework for the future of healthcare and a roadmap for how to navigate through it, this book also incorporates hundreds of examples of companies actually building this blueprint. You will be provided specific examples of how, as patients, you can get the most out of this new delivery system. This book also includes sections that make it very practical:

1. **Patient Stories**–provide real-life examples of how people use technologies to improve their health experience.
2. **44 Insider Tips**–offer practical takeaways from each chapter.
3. **List of Promising Startups**–allows you to find the latest companies transforming healthcare. **Over 250 different companies and technologies** are discussed in this book.
4. **Condition Specific**–coverage of over 13 different medical conditions–the last chapter gives examples by condition (diabetes, pregnancy, etc.).

Let's start by taking a peek at how the new future will look and the important principles to understand in this digital age of medicine.

The first section, *digital revolution*, provides an important overview of the key premises that are transforming healthcare. It discusses what approaches and factors will lead us to faster, better, smarter and lower cost care.

The second section, *digital prevention*, discusses in detail the prescription to having the right mindset and how to use digital technologies to prevent and pre-empt illness.

The third section, *digital optimization*, goes into how to improve your care if you have a medical condition or become ill. It will discuss how you can take better care of your children and your older parents. It provides shortcuts, tips, and an approach to making sure you can make the best decisions in the shortest time.

*****

Disclaimer: In this book, a number of companies, products, and technologies are mentioned. They are primarily used for illustrative purposes; and also because they embody the very essence of why and how healthcare is changing. No company has provided compensation to have its product, services, or technology included.

And given the rapid change in the industry, my review is not exhaustive nor a "top ten" list. In fact, **many companies will fail and some that are included have already failed!** I've chosen to leave them in, in part to showcase the difficult nature of the changing industry, and to highlight all the hard work of some early pioneers.

SECTION I:

DIGITAL REVOLUTION

1

CEO OF YOUR HEALTH

Y ou wake up one morning in the not so distant future after a fun evening at your company party. You're coughing, sneezing, and shivering with chills and a fever. *Oh no. What do I have? How bad is this going to get? Should I go to work and risk getting everyone else sick, or stay home? Do I need to see the doctor for this? Will I get better on my own?*

You used to have to take a gamble when making such decisions. But in the not so distant future, you won't have to answer those questions based solely on your gut feelings.

Instead, you turn on your iPad and go to your doctor's virtual office. You "ping" her and let her know you're feeling sick. She gets on a video chat and asks you to check your pulse and temperature. She recommends you go to the *diagnostic ATM* (dATM) at the local pharmacy and have yourself checked out.

Fortunately for you, there's a pharmacy just down the block equipped with a dATM. Imagine a machine similar to a Redbox that has medical services built in. The dATM is equipped with an electronic reader so all you have to do is swipe your cellphone to securely transfer health information. Your cellphone provides the dATM with your medical records and instructions from your physician. The machine dispenses a sterile Q-tip, you swab your nose, you put the swab into a plastic case, and the case then goes into the slot in the dATM. The process will be similar to returning a movie at a Redbox. The dATM also takes a picture of your throat and listens to your lungs.

While you're waiting for your nose swab to be processed, you also review your doctor's recommendations on your cellphone. Based on your fever symptoms, she suggests you buy elderberry lozenges, ibuprofen, and lots of Smart Water.

The dATM processes the sample and within minutes delivers lab results directly to your doctor's patient management program, which sends her an alert. She accesses the results from her phone which, in conjunction with the information you provided earlier from your iPad, provide her enough information to make a diagnosis.

In a few minutes, you receive a text message on your phone with the results of your swab test. You have a viral infection— influenza! The text message also includes a prescription for an anti-viral medication, which has already been sent to the pharmacy so you can start therapy right away.

With all of that information on your cellphone, you walk up to an "automated prescription dispensing" machine and wave your phone's barcode at the reader. The machine drops a pre-packaged Tamiflu. The dispensing machine texts you a link to a video that explains when and how often to take those pills.

Your doctor also sets up a text message reminder so that you know exactly what to do over the next 24 hours. She schedules a follow-up online chat in 48 hours in which you will discuss your progress.

You go back home. Call your boss. You tell him you just confirmed you have the flu but still can work from home. Your boss is really happy that you're not going to come in and potentially expose your colleagues. "Just work from home all week," he says, "if you are feeling up to it."

Welcome to the **future of healthcare delivery!** Break all your assumptions of how you will access, engage, and receive care. As I explain later, these coordinated and efficient interactions will drive a patient-provider dynamic that will be more patient-centered than physician-centered.

This changing dynamic will inevitably make you more involved with your own care, and more financially responsible as well! To this end, we are all becoming CEOs of our health. We will need to make health related decisions (versus solely relying on physicians), and we will increasingly be more involved with **budgeting, planning, and making investments at it relates to our health.**

For some, I think this could be a remarkably frustrating era in healthcare, as each of us has to weigh the benefits of care versus costs. But I think given today's digital tools, there is an opportunity to be both more engaged in the process as well as to live healthier, disease free lives!

Patients Co-Pilot Care

In principle, it seems simple enough **to upskill patients into better decision makers, co-pilots, and partners.** In tomorrow's world, we will have the technology to truly activate patients like never before. But will patients want this responsibility? How will they grasp the terminology and nuances of medicine? Doesn't it take years of training for a doctor to grasp this information? Will they *want* to be the CEO of their own health?

In fact, we have the opposite doctor-patient dynamic now. Our system sometimes infantilizes patients and some doctors inadvertently worsen this by talking down to patients. As a country, we spend very few dollars on true patient education. The medical literacy deficit is one of the key reasons nearly $300 billion[4] of expense goes to waste each year. If patients feel that they cannot engage, don't understand what their doctors say, and are not given time to ask questions, then this disconnect creates a huge sinkhole of medical waste.

As an ER doc, I see this all the time—people who have horribly worn-out bodies. I see them after diabetes has destroyed their nerves, eyes, and kidneys. I see them after heart disease makes it difficult to breathe or even walk. By the time I see them, all that we can do amounts to applying Band-Aids to a gaping wound. These patients will never be quite the same again. There is no way to repair their tissue and organs to the extent that is necessary to re-establish "normalcy."

Patients come in with high blood pressure, for example, and have no idea that eating salty fast foods on a daily basis is a significant problem. The following is a typical conversation I may have with a patient:

Patient: I am not sure why my blood pressure is so high. I take my meds, but it's still 220/120.

Me: What do you usually eat?

Patient: I have switched to chicken because I read it is healthier.

Me: Okay. What and where do you usually eat?

Patient: You know, the usual: Carl's Jr., Taco Bell, and KFC. It takes too much time to cook.

This patient is, unfortunately, one I encounter frequently. It's all too common for patients to have little information on how their choices can impact their health. That fast food is often an incredibly high source of sodium. That most patients could very easily be eating several times the daily recommended amount of sodium just by eating out once. Ironically, this conversation at times happens while patients are nibbling on potato chips (that they find in ER waiting room vending machines) or fast food (brought in by their family members). Overall, we need to expect more from patients and from ourselves when it comes to our own health. We need to **proactively think about how our behaviors impact our health**. The good news is that new technologies are providing **not only a solution, but also a patient revolution**.

Insider Tips

1. **We are in a different era of medicine!** You can have a much greater impact on your health than at *any other time in history*.

2. **Don't expect all your health needs to get addressed solely by a single doctor.** Given the explosion of scientific knowledge, it's not practical or realistic today to assume that your doctor will know it all. You need to be an active co-pilot.

Empowerment Is Inevitable

If you don't believe me, let me share with you below how some large forces are working together to push you into greater decision-making roles.

Healthcare is becoming more rationed. As I mentioned earlier, most primary care doctors only have 7 to 10 minutes twice a year to spend with each patient. The doctor may focus on a key medical issue while nurses and other providers fill in the gaps and handle other important tasks. With so many people involved, these processes may be disjointed and more prone to error. That leaves patients to integrate it all, which isn't an easy task. So as Smart Patients, we must be willing to take ownership of the process in a way that provides us with the best care.

Healthcare is becoming more specialized. Many patients still want to go to just one doctor to get all of their questions answered, but this model is becoming increasingly difficult to sustain. One doctor will no longer be able to know everything. Some of this is due to the increasingly complex nature of technology within specific specialty areas. Some orthopedic surgeons, for example, are now required to have special hand surgeon training due to the complexity of the hand and the number of new, cutting edge procedures involved. So your doctor may not be trained enough in carpal tunnel treatments of the hand, for example, and send you to a specialist.

Healthcare is becoming more checklist driven. Although some authorities argue the need for having doctors check a box to indicate that they have performed an activity, this does not give doctors an incentive to do anything other than what's on the list! For example, if doctors are busy checking boxes, they may not think "outside the box" (or have enough time) to ask about your recent travel to Liberia and your possible exposure to Ebola. I can guarantee you that electronic medical records (EMRs) did not have a checkbox for Ebola risk before the outbreak in the US. Patients must understand that a doctor's focus might be **consumed by process overload**, and they will need to inform doctors of significant life events that could have a bearing on their clinical decision making.

So what should you do as the 'CEO of Your Health'? You would:

1. Prioritize your **health goals** and have a **health game plan** as you age.
2. **Proactively check** for new apps, devices, diagnostics, and websites that can help you manage your own health.
3. Learn how to **make investments in your health** that will pay off in the future. Care is only going to get more expensive. The sooner you start to think about creating a financial plan for your healthcare over the next few decades, the better off you will be.

The remainder of this book dives into taking advantage of digital innovations. And if you have the inclination, this knowledge will allow you to become a great CEO.

Now that I have established that we all need to take a leadership role in our health, let's look more tactically at what are the prescriptions that will drive this personal health revolution.

2

PRESCRIPTION FOR CHANGE

O ur current model of health is not known for speed. Patients call to make an appointment and usually wait for weeks; then they get to the waiting room and often wait hours to finally see the doctor, and then get sent to a lab; then wait weeks for another appointment—just to get the results. This is probably why we call our customers "patients"—they have to be patient!

It's even worse in the ER. Patients typically show up and wait 4 to 6 hours to spend about 15 minutes to talk to me. It is embarrassing to work inside a system like this.

As mentioned in the first chapter, healthcare has traditionally pivoted around the doctor. Until recently, if you wanted care, you needed to:

1. make an appointment
2. get in your car or take the bus to go see the doctor

3. have the doctor evaluate you and order tests
4. go to the lab to get the tests
5. make a follow-up appointment with the doctor to review the test results
6. and often get a referral to a specialist

It takes 5 to 6 steps just to get basic blood work done. That's a lot of time away from work—or childcare responsibilities—to get relatively routine medical care.

However, that's clearly changing. Healthcare is beginning to pivot around the patient. And it's about time—literally! Patients can now email their doctor or chat with them online. They can do online research to get basic health information from someone other than their doctor. They can find healthcare outlets in pharmacies, malls, at work, or just by searching Google. Behind this paradigm shift is a fundamental change in the doctor-patient relationship. You will need to champion this transformation.

Insider Tips

3. **Understand the digital options you now have to get healthcare** e.g., at work, online, etc.

4. **Don't be afraid to get in deep with medical topics**—there are plenty of resources to help tutor you.

Different Doctors

These new models ask doctors to evolve as well. In these models, doctors may be called upon to **analyze data that is delivered** differently, and often in the form of electronic communication, such as email and chat, or activity trackers like Fitbit. Doctors will get more contextual data on how their patients live, eat, work, and play.

Sharing will also be different. Previously, doctors wrote difficult-to-read notes on paper. Now they must use an EMR. Next it will be entering information into a patient's health portal and working with a patient's care team. As Smart Patients, we need to encourage this evolution of "doctoring."

Different Patients

Since we all one day will become patients, as an entire country we will need to make different choices. By thinking about health as a **series of mini-transactions**, like going to the bank or dry cleaners, we will increasingly be able to access care on our own schedule. On-demand healthcare allows patients to get specific services, like a blood pressure check, vaccine shot, prescription for travel medications, or a test for HIV, without having to go through a traditional medical process.

Moreover, Smart Patients *won't "save up" their health issues* and expect to have them addressed in a single seven-minute consultation with a physician.

From this perspective, healthcare is actually shrinking into these **faster bite-sized transactions.** This fundamental shift in mindset will allow for a more efficient health organization to develop.

Different Experiences

Ultimately, many of us desire a different health experience. The remainder of this chapter will discuss four themes critical to changing our health experience and driving it to be faster, better, smarter, and cheaper.

Digital Impact #1:
Faster...Distributed, On-Demand Health Delivery

When I talk about faster, I am talking about faster time to diagnosis, to therapy, to *specific* **healthcare transactions you require**, and ultimately to a successful outcome. Faster is something we all want because we have a feeling that it takes too long to get the health answers we want.

But how do we get to this model of healthcare? It starts with a transformation similar to what has happened in banking and other industries—where accessing healthcare becomes distributed. We used to go to banks to get cash; now we go to ATMs. These automated tellers are smart machines that help us perform fundamental services. But they don't do everything. When we need more advanced services, like mortgage services, then we still go to a bank branch. This idea of using a **right-sized, distributed model** is key to making healthcare faster.

Start With Simple Bite-Sized Steps
Again, think of care as **a number of simple steps or transactions** (such as getting a flu shot, blood pressure check, etc.). In the years to come, these steps will become increasingly available on demand, at a push of a button, and distributed in new, unexpected locations. These procedures will be handled by people who are medically trained, but *who may not carry the mantle of medical doctor*. In some cases, they may be carried out by specialized technologies, which are discussed later in more detail.

Allow Care To Happen Everywhere
Lower-cost and right-sized care will allow for procedures to occur in places that we would have never expected to see them,

in smaller chunks, and at the convenience of patients. This is already happening with mini-clinics (like Take Care at Walgreens and Minute Clinic at CVS) in pharmacy stores. Among other innovations, the future of healthcare delivery will likely push us past pharmacy clinics toward care kiosks, such as diagnostic ATMs that can tell us if we are sick without requiring human intervention.

Provide Patients A Care Navigator

Smartphones (and other mobile devices such as tablets, smart watches, smart glasses, and smart clothing) will become our **digital health assistants**. They will navigate us through healthcare much like our car's GPS—it can get us to the right location in the shortest distance and time. This platform will identify which outlets will bring the most value for our money. These digital assistants will also take on the burden of keeping up-to-date on health issues.

Digital Impact #2:
Better...Early Warning, Pre-Emptive Interventions

By better, I am arguing that our system could **identify disease and illness earlier and intervene**. Better stops disease dead in its tracks before it has time to damage our **cells, organs, and bodies**. Better means that we **won't develop diseases** such as heart disease, diabetes, Alzheimer's, cancer, etc., but better will require a **different medical mindset and proactive patients**.

This emerging area is called **pre-emptive medicine.** This is different from preventive medicine, which seeks to prevent diseases at the population level (typically through behavioral recommendations or mass immunizations).

Create A Weather Channel For Your Health

Many of us are daily weather checkers. But do we do the same for the "weather in our bodies"? We, in fact, have a constantly changing internal weather system that can change from moment to moment.

So when I talk about better, it starts with understanding that we need a "weather" **surveillance system for our cells and organs.** It can alert us when storms are approaching so we can prepare. In the coming years, technologies will increasingly be able to identify early warning signs and pre-disease states.

For you, it means a total rethink of how we should manage our bodies and engage with doctors. Given the rate of innovation, many doctors may not be up to speed on every new company, technology, or trend. You will need to coach your doctors and identify the latest ways to self-screen for a number of diseases, especially if you have a family history of a particular disease.

As mentioned, early warning or pre-emptive health is different from prevention. The latter offers general guidelines for individuals regardless of whether they will contract a disease or not. It's a bit like wearing a raincoat *during the entire month* of April, because statistically, it rains a lot in April. A better system will know exactly when your body needs a "raincoat," and when it can go without.

I am not arguing that we should live in fear or become hypochondriacs, worried about every ache and pain. In fact, these new technologies will **take out much of the guesswork and "wait and see" attitude.**

Stop Disease Dead In Its Tracks...Well Before Symptoms
Pre-emptive care, like umbrellas on rainy days, will avert damage from a patient's body at a time when it could be most effective to do so.

This is critical because most **diseases show up in our cells well before any symptoms occur.** But our current system is almost entirely based on the patient having a symptom (such as chest pain or cough, for instance) and then working to find the cause. However, by the time a patient has symptoms, the disease process—in most cases—has already become well entrenched in the body.

Take Alzheimer's dementia, for example, which involves progressive damage to brain cells. Using current protocols to detect it, even in its earliest stages, it is generally too late because a significant number of brain cells have already been lost. Even if we were able to stop the disease at that point, too much irreversible damage has often already occurred. What we need is a way to detect the onset of diseases way *before* any damage has occurred. This means we cannot wait for, or rely on, the current signs-and-symptoms checker to start screening patients for diseases. Only by **detecting diseases at a cellular level will we be able to administer therapies at the optimal time**—giving them the best chance to work.

Digital Impact #3: Smarter...Individualized Technologies, Therapies, And Treatments

With smarter, I am referring to having a system that is **adaptive and personalized to who we are.** I think most of us feel that healthcare can be somewhat impersonal and confusing. We get generic recommendations like "cut out salt." We don't often understand what doctors tell us. The smarter revolution is about you demanding that hospitals and doctors act to **create a plan that is specific to you.**

Make Care Tailored To You And Your Genetics

The digital age of medicine means technologies, therapies, and treatments will fit your unique physiology, DNA, gender, and culture. We are moving from a model in which doctors prescribe medications that work on the average patient toward one in which doctors will be able to prescribe customized **medications that will work with your specific chemistry.** This will lead to improved outcomes and fewer unwanted side effects. "One size fits all" healthcare (which has never fit anyone very well) is over. This **digital customization** will lead to better adoption and compliance by patients, ultimately driving down costs. Smart Patients **must demand this level of personalization and precision medicine**.

Deliver Care On Patients' Terms

Physicians are notorious for speaking in "doctor talk." In fact, many studies show that **patients only remember about 15% of what a doctor tells them.** Can you imagine a system where 85% of "medical value" gets lost in translation? This huge value leak happens in the majority of clinics and hospitals.

Thankfully, numerous companies are transforming how the system is engaging with patients to make it truly on the terms of the patient—whether it's making health recommendations fit a patient's food preference, attitudes toward exercise, or the best ways to stay motivated.

Digital Impact #4:
Cheaper...Efficient, Networked Powered Care

When I talk about cheaper, I am talking about how you will have access to the right information at the right time, and how you will be directed to **the right care at the right price and value**. This does not mean that you will get low-quality healthcare that is "cheap."

When I hear of the medical bills my patients get from the ER, it is simply scary. And as a doctor, it is somewhat embarrassing when patients ask me questions about it. Should an MRI that takes 15 minutes really cost $3,000? But when a doctor resuscitates someone who is about to die, they get about $350 from most insurers! Costs, in our system, often don't truly reflect the value created by the doctor, drug, hospital, etc.

There are a lot of smart people—economists and policy makers—working on this issue at the macro level, so this book will not discuss issues like why the list price for an MRI is more expensive in the US than just about anywhere else in the world.

Rather, this book focuses on patient empowerment. There are two relatively **new digital concepts in healthcare**: *transparency* and *network effects*, both of which can drive down costs and get you more bang for your healthcare buck. While this may be intuitive to most people—more information leads to better decisions at a lower expense—there are powerful new shifts happening that will dramatically change our health behaviors in a networked environment. And behavior change will ultimately lower costs by driving down demand. Information and how we engage with information will be the critical stepping-stone in getting us to better health.

Let The Network "See You Now"

We all know the power of networks. Just look to Facebook and Twitter. We know the value of easily finding information when we search for plane tickets on Kayak or placing bids on Priceline. The same types of platforms and networks are starting to show up in healthcare.

We will be able to get better deals. In business lingo, this is called **price transparency or value transparency**; e.g., the ability to know the cost of knee replacement before the surgery (price) or the ability to know that an expensive cancer drug will work (value). Getting more transparency is perhaps the most critical element in lowering healthcare costs.

Efficiencies will also emerge through better communication and collaboration among the major players in the system: hospitals, insurers, providers, and public health. This ecosystem will become more interconnected, increasing the exchange of information, data, and knowledge. This is also called the *network effect*, which will ultimately lead to more efficient and "cheaper" care.

Tap Into Patient-Powered Care

Patients themselves can **be a great source to lower costs.** For example, Smart Patients will also connect with each other through patient networks to share knowledge about all aspects of care such as how to prevent medication side effects, which can lower the cost to manage complications.

Patients will also be empowered to safely take care of themselves. For example, innovations that allow patients to safely self-triage to the right provider (ER vs. Urgent Care) could be one quick and easy way to lower the costs in the system.

*****

As the chapter title describes, the "prescription for change" asks all parts of the healthcare system—patients, doctors, hospitals, payers, med techs—**to take steps to change the way medical engagement occurs**. It also asks for a mind shift in thinking about how to use the right resources at the right time, finding solutions to pre-empt disease, using more precise recommendations to improve therapy effectiveness, and using the power of networks to help us lower costs. Now I want to provide an overview of how to create an action plan so you can get faster, better, smarter, and lower cost care.

3

YOUR DIGITAL GAME PLAN

L et's face it—most of us wish we could avoid the doctor altogether. We would rather be running, eating out, and watching Netflix. Managing health, for most of us, has become fairly reactive. Most of us exercise because we have gained a few pounds over Christmas. Many of us eat willy-nilly until we find out that we have developed diabetes. But now, because we all share in the increasing cost of healthcare, it has become a financial imperative to have a plan.

With new digital tools, as described in this book, it is now easier to create and stick to a plan. This is what I recommend:

1. **Get the right team.** Find digitally savvy doctors, health plans, hospitals, and other providers. Or coach your doctor to become one!

2. **Have a portfolio of options.** Identify tools, technologies, and services that will enable you to succeed and achieve your goals.

3. **Think short-term and long-term.** There are lots of technologies that can help you and your family today. But also understand how pre-emptive technologies can make sure you have a long and healthy life.

4. **Become a better healthcare shopper.** It will be important to know how to use the Internet and patient networks to find a lower-cost medication, CT or MRI, or medical center for a hip surgery. More on this in later chapters.

5. **Stay in the game.** Take the lead on staying up-to-date. Subscribe to email newsletters that can keep you informed on the latest advances in asthma, diabetes, heart disease, etc. Partner with your doctor to identify the right technologies. There are also some newsletters and websites in the appendix to consider.

Insider Tips

5. **Develop a game plan to engage with digital health innovations**—before you get sick.

6. **Innovations can both prevent and optimize your healthcare**—learn about both perspectives when reading this book.

You can also create a digital game plan, framed around the themes of faster, better, smarter, and cheaper. For example, a game plan might look like:

- *Faster* – when you think you have the flu, **get a telemedical consult** on your phone so you can get **the right care sooner.**

- *Better* – ask your doctors for **diagnostics that can help screen you** for cardiac or diabetic disease well before you develop the disease outright.

- *Smarter* – **find apps or services** that will help your doctor provide tailored treatments that work for your weight goals, eating preferences, etc.

- *Cheaper* – **use web tools** to get lower-cost medications or **log into medical communities** where you can learn from others with your condition.

A Closer Look At The Digital Health Revolution

The revolution will allow you to have access to a broad range of new resources so you can create an individualized and effective plan to improve your health. These topics are covered in greater detail throughout the book. Below are a few online resources that illustrate what a digital health game plan can do for you.

- **Weight loss – Spark People** is the largest online community for weight loss. Users can achieve weight loss goals by tracking their food intake and workouts, and documenting weigh-ins. In addition, users connect with other members to provide support, share dieting tips, and swap healthy recipes (sparkpeople.com).

- **Screen for heart disease and diabetes – Cardiodx** provides a simple blood test that can help determine if that subtle pain in your chest is actually a blocked heart vessel (cardiodx.com). **Boston Heart Labs** also provides proprietary screening tests that can help you predict your risk for diabetes and heart disease (bostonheartdiagnostics.com).

- **Lower prescriptions costs and hospital bills – GoodRx** compares the costs of getting prescription drugs at different pharmacies. Many pharmacies have different prices for the same drugs and prices can vary as much as 50%. It pays to check this site before getting a prescription filled (goodrx.com). And to better understand the cost difference between hospitals and medical procedures, try **NerdWallet** or **Guroo,** which provide an estimated cost of getting a surgery or other procedures (nerdwallet.com, guroo.com).

- **Better grocery shopping – GoodGuide** provides rankings of foods and other products based on whether they're safe, healthy, "green," or socially responsible (goodguide.com).

- **Know where to go – Symcat** is a diagnostic tool that allows you to input your symptoms, demographics, and medical history. Then, using that information, it generates a list of possible diagnoses with recommendations of where to go for medical care (symcat.com).

- **If your kid has ear pain – Cellscope** offers a device that attaches to your smartphone and can send photos of the eardrum to a doctor. Imagine not taking time off from work to take your kid into the pediatrician's office (cellscope.com).

- **Engage with a nutritionist virtually – Mobile Food Coach** connects people with certified nutrition coaches to make sure they are making healthy food choices. Simply take photos of your meals each day and your assigned coach gives you real time advice and tips (mobilefoodcoach.com).

A Day In The Life Of An Asthma Patient

To make the idea of getting a digital health game plan clearer, let's take an example of an asthma patient: Tom. Each day he has to perform a number of jobs to manage his asthma, such as take daily medications, typically a steroid inhaler; measure his wheeze state with a peak flow meter; avoid environmental triggers; and be aware of the pollen count. He also needs a flu vaccine each year.

Tom is a busy sales guru and doesn't want to get slowed down, so he is very concerned about preventing flare-ups. When he does get a flare, he wants to recover quickly—like most of us. So Tom has digital tools. He has an app that tells him a daily pollen count and weather systems that are entering the area that could cause a flare. He bought a peak flow meter, which he connects to his smartphone and uses weekly. This information is sent to his doctor via the Cloud and an alert is created if Tom is in a trouble zone. When he gets a flare-up, he has a digital stethoscope (developed by AirSonea), that attaches to his phone and can record his breathing. His doctor can listen to it on the other end during a telemedicine visit.

Tom is taking advantage of digital prevention and digital optimization. Like asthma, many other conditions we cover in this book, will be transformed through digital technologies.

Digital Revolution Summary

All in all, there are hundreds of new innovations that are emerging to help empower patients with new digital tools, diagnostics, and devices—driving the themes of faster, better, smarter, and cheaper healthcare. As you read this book, I hope you take notes so you can build out a digital health game plan. There is **a page at the end of this section** to help you do that.

The remainder of the book outlines the game plan organized into ways most people think about health:

- **How do I stay healthy** (digital prevention)?
- **What do I do if I get sick** (digital optimization)?

Here are these important concepts in more detail:

1. **Digital Prevention** – is about learning how and when to use digital tools so you can stay healthy.

    I will introduce you to **early warning sensors** and **pre-emptive diagnostics** to find the signs of disease and halt disease progression. You will become skilled at using tools to **improve your memory and overall health status**. Learn when to **add alarms** to your body to get real time data. Identify ways to **use your own cells** to repair damaged ones. Seek treatments that are unique to your body. Complement your care with alternative therapies such as yoga, meditation, and acupuncture in conjunction with traditional medicine. This section of the book will jumpstart you into using these tools to manage your health proactively.

2. **Digital Optimization** – we are all eventually going to get sick, as we age. And when we do, we should know how to best manage the process, at the lowest cost in terms of time and dollars.

    For example, you can **learn about getting second opinions** at major medical centers without leaving your home. Get help **preparing for the physician visit** and use tools that can help you remember what the doctor said. Learn about **when to go to an ER, urgent care, PCP or other online resource.** Overall, I believe that with the right tools, the healthcare experience can be almost painless, and I will teach you how.

I hope this book will help guide you and your family to a better health experience and take advantage of emerging opportunities to stay well. We all deserve this promise.

Your Digital Health Game Plan

(best filled out after you read the book)

What are your health goals?

_____

_____

Faster – what apps, websites, devices can make your care faster?

1. _____

2. _____

3. _____

Better – what diagnostic tests, apps, and devices can help you get screened for the right conditions to pre-empt disease?

1. _____

2. _____

3. _____

Smarter – what technologies can make your treatments more customized?

1. _____

2. _____

3. _____

Cheaper – what tools and networks are available that can lower your care costs?

1. _____

2. _____

3. _____

SECTION II:

DIGITAL PREVENTION

4

FIND A DIGITALLY SAVVY DOCTOR

Finding the right doctor can be a challenge. As part of the interview process, it's important to learn how open your doctor is to new digital and diagnostic technologies. It could make your life easier—imagine emailing or texting your doctor, or seeing your doctor on Skype instead of trekking to the clinic. Typically, these doctors will also be open to discussing with you information you find online.

To illustrate this, let's look at David, who is turning 42 and is starting to think about his health more. He has a complicated family history. His uncle has Parkinson's. His grandfather has heart disease. His cousin developed colon cancer at an early age.

Having heard about digital health, David finds a website where he can search for a doctor who is digitally savvy. After an online chat with this doctor—Dr. Digital—he realizes that this is a great fit for him. Dr. Digital uses email, video chat, and an online engagement platform to remind and encourage patients. This works great for David because he is a sales rep who travels making in person appointments difficult to keep.

David learns from this doctor that he can also get screened for Parkinson's, colon cancer, and heart disease all with a simple blood test. He takes these blood tests and finds out that he has an increased risk for getting heart disease but an average risk for both Parkinson's disease and colon cancer, so he is relieved given his family history.

His doctor gives him a device that he can wear (at least once a year) that will monitor his heart to detect the earliest signs of heart disease. He also enrolls in a food coaching program and workout plan specifically designed to improve heart health. David feels empowered and understands his role in shaping his health destiny. He has found the perfect doctor for him.

As you know, finding the right doctor has some trial and error in the process. It is important to review traditional factors—where they were trained, their views on pre-emptive medicine, their bedside manner, etc. I have outlined a few more tips that can potentially help you find a digitally savvy doc:

1. **Read through the doctor's website.** Just perusing the physician's website will tell you a lot about how important they find technology and what sort of role it plays in their practice. They will often discuss the use of email and other communication tools.

2. **Interview the office manager.** This is a way to "vet" the office before committing to the practice and helps avoid a

"blind date" with your doc. Does the doctor have online videos or podcasts? Do they suggest any good websites or apps for patients to use as resources? Do they update their practice regularly to reflect the latest research and recommendations? These types of questions can serve as a barometer to let you know whether this is a practice you should consider.

3. **Set up an appointment (some may even Skype you).** If you are happy with your findings from the above two tasks, talk to the doctor. Ask them about what types of tools they use to communicate with patients, if they have video appointments, and their approach to using innovative diagnostics and devices (which are covered later). Ask about specific tests and alternative therapies that interest you. This process can help ensure that your relationship with the doctor and their office will be a good fit.

Insider Tips

7. **Learn to become a healthcare shopper**—it is a relatively new phenomena, but you must learn about finding the best value for your dollar.

8. **Find a team that is digitally empowered**—start up a conversation with your doctor on how he or she uses innovations in their practice.

Digital Checkup

A new type of checkup is on the horizon. This checkup will include the same components, but **will be coordinated and done remotely in discrete steps**.

Appointments will be carried out via videoconference; paperwork will be completed online and submitted ahead of time. Digital checkups will also be more in depth, collecting more information in a shorter amount of time, using more sophisticated devices and smart apps. Vital signs will be collected with your smartphone with the help of some nifty device extensions.

A single drop of blood will reveal elements such as blood glucose, inflammatory markers, and genetics. These samples could be dropped off at a mobile lab or sent in by mail. These results will all be saved to a secure system, using your smartphone or tablet as a platform, and can easily be shared in real time with your doctor.

For a patient in his 20s or 30s, a **virtualized appointment** might include a screening for cancer markers and diabetes. In an older patient, a checkup would include analysis of the patient's heart rhythm and risk for developing heart disease. The possibilities are endless and exciting!

Become A Healthcare Shopper

To be a Smart Patient means that you also need to become a **savvy shopper**, which will also help you find a great doctor. To bring this to life, let's imagine that in the future, getting health services will be as simple as shopping on Amazon. Let's take a look at a hypothetical patient named Brian.

He's a runner, and lately it has been too painful to run so he thinks maybe he has injured his knee. Brian's doctor tells him, "You need to get an MRI," and also says, "Here is a website to find the lowest-priced place to go."

In this case, Brian does a simple online search and finds a complete price list from hospitals and imaging centers in his area—everything is laid out, from the technician's fee to the cost of transferring the image to a CD. All of this information enables him to shop around and find the best deal. Since these prices are advertised and readily available, local providers of a service will have to compete for a patient's business, keeping prices low. Brian is able to set up an MRI at the center closest to his work and even gets a discount by mentioning that a center across town is $200 less.

Brain has a torn meniscus and will likely need surgery. He finds a number of orthopedic doctors who will review his case online through a "second opinion" website (which is discussed later) and has a video chat with the doctor. After going through this process, Brian feels very confident that he has chosen the right doctor and that he can get back to running.

Find A Digital Doctor

Most people find primary care doctors by looking on their insurance card and calling around to find the earliest appointment.

Patients may inquire about years in practice, training, or clinic hours. There are now many sites that will help you find doctors online. These may only provide names and pedigree, but I thought I should list them regardless. You still have some homework, and as a Smart Patient, you need to learn to ask:

- Does the doctor respond to emails?

- Can I send the doctor texts or picture messages?

- Does the doctor have a blog?

- Does the doctor use videos to help me learn?

Finding these doctors may take a little legwork, but in the long run will make your life a lot easier. To get names of providers here are a few suggestions:

- Your insurance provider portal
- Healthgrades.com
- DocSpot.com
- Vitals.com
- ZocDoc.com
- Healthtap.com

To engage in digital prevention, you need to start by **finding the right team.** And this might be your current doctor. In fact, many doctors and hospitals are starting to launch digital strategies and patient engagement tools. In the next chapter I show you how to use apps to stay healthy.

5

AN APP A DAY...
KEEPS YOUR DOCTOR AWAY

oing to the App Store and searching for health apps might be as important as going for your annual physical! I say that partially in jest, but in reality the impact of health apps can be profound. We all use them but the trick is to actively assemble a portfolio of health apps that will work for you.

No single app will cover all your health needs. And each person will need a different collection of apps. Also, as you get older, your health needs will change. You may get married and become pregnant. If your kid has asthma, you'll want an app that will track his asthma status. If you have chronic health issues such as diabetes or heart disease, you may want an app to organize those important conversations you have with your doctor. So the **right collection of apps for you will change over time**.

To this end, they will continue to transform how doctors will engage with patients and how quickly you can access care—from getting answers to simple questions to receiving virtual care right over the phone. Many hospitals, and even physicians, will have their own apps delivering a whole new consumer-driven experience. Also, they are being used in clinical studies to actually measure their benefits. One study, done with Weight Watchers patients, showed motivational text messages provided a statistically significant weight loss (4.5 more pounds lost) than those without the messaging feature.[5]

What makes an app different from just going online for healthcare (to a website like WebMD) is that the app uses some feature of your phone that **can't easily be done through a web browser.** For example, an app (like Fooducate) might use your camera to scan a barcode and deliver health information right in a grocery store.

At the time this book was written, the Apple App Store offered over 50,000 health related ones all fueled by consumer interest and that number is growing daily. In fact, the trajectory of users embracing health apps is staggering. Juniper, a research firm, estimates that there will be 142 million health app downloads in 2016. Eventually, **doctors will prescribe apps along with, or in place of, drugs for many common conditions**—they may ask, "Would you like an app for that?"

Insider Tips

9. **Finding the right app takes experimentation**—spend a little time looking through the apps in this book, and many others can be found on Itunes and Google Play.

10. **Stay ahead and hack your health**—even if you don't have any significant medical issues, apps can help keep you fit and healthy.

You may already use them. In fact, 95 million mobile users have used apps for healthcare, according to the PEW research group. What may be surprising is the breadth of smartphone app uses:

- remotely diagnosing acute appendicitis
- detecting melanoma
- pinpointing outbreaks of malaria
- substituting for microscopes, stethoscopes, otoscopes, and ophthalmoscopes
- tracking heart rhythms
- monitoring our babies' feeding habits

In fact, studies by Telenor/The Boston Consulting Group highlight that mobile health apps can reduce the cost of elder care by 25%, reduce maternal and perinatal mortality by 30%, enable twice as many rural patients to be reached per physician, and boost medical compliance because 30% of smartphone users are likely to use wellness apps.[6]

Mobile apps provide a way to get and track information on the fly. For example, you can store questions you have for your doctor and record key points of a doctor's visit in the same app, so you'll never forget what you wanted to ask and what your doctor told you! Check out HealthVoiceApp.com, a password protected app that I developed to help my patients remember key points from their visits.

As I mentioned, innovation is happening fast and it is important to conduct your own research to stay current. There are a number of large companies and startups that are creating health related apps.

Below are some useful ones worth checking out. But more importantly, I want to give you a sense of the wonderful things to expect from **doing your own homework** on finding the best ones for you.

Eating Better

- **Fooducate** helps you **"grade" your food** purchases by scanning the package barcode. It can quickly help you get nutritional information and informs you if a food you scanned is high in fat, cholesterol, sodium, or if it contains GMOs so you can buy the highest quality food. It also offers a platform for you to track what you've eaten each day as well as any physical activity you have completed (fooducate.com).

- **Shopwell** allows you to input your grocery list and offers an overall health "score" for each item. Scan a package's barcode and learn about what's in the product you selected. It also offers healthier alternatives to help you maintain your nutrition goals (shopwell.com).

- **TellSpec** has developed a unique pocket-sized food-sensor scanner that identifies calories, ingredients, chemicals, and allergens in food to help you understand what is in the foods you are consuming (tellspec.com).

- **Loseit** helps you lose weight by tracking both exercise and calories. You select a target weight for yourself and the amount of weight you want to lose each week. The program adjusts to set your caloric budget so you can make smarter food choices. The database includes many chain restaurants, national grocery stores, and food items (loseit.com).

Preventing Food Allergies

- **Grain or No Grain** educates you about gluten. Test your gluten knowledge by taking a quiz, learn about safe and unsafe foods, and review which restaurant menu items are gluten-free when you are dining out (grainornograin.com).

- **Allergy Caddy, Foods You Can, & MyFoodFacts** take the guesswork out of what types of hidden allergens are in restaurant food. Allergy Caddy, for example, includes information on the top 10 allergens/sensitivities and has data for 40 fast food restaurants. It's a tool for translating a restaurant's food-allergy guide to your specific needs (allergycaddy.com, foodsyoucan.com, myfoodfacts.com).

Cancer Screening

- **SkinVision & UMSkinCheck from the University of Michigan** allow for self-exam and surveillance of suspicious moles that could turn into cancerous melanomas (uofmhealth.org). Both allow you to take pictures of your moles and get feedback and find a skin specialist. Skinvision provides an activity map of areas with the highest risk and incidence of skin cancer (skinvision.org).

- **Pink Bra** walks you through a step-by-step process of how to do a breast self-exam, allows you to set weekly or monthly reminders to perform exams, and ultimately allows women to be proactive in early breast cancer detection. Find this on iTunes.

Better Sleep

- **Sleepbot** uses motion sensors to track your sleep patterns and gently wakes you up at the stage of sleep that you need to be woken up. It also uses sound monitoring to see if sounds in your environment affect how well you sleep (mysleepbot.com).

- **Sleep Cycle** measures as you go from light sleep to deep sleep. This "bio-alarm clock" uses motion sensors to track your movements while you're asleep, estimates what stage of sleep you're in, and wakes you up in your lightest sleep phase (sleepcycle.com).

Conceiving And Having A Healthy Pregnancy

- **Mobile Mom** (mobilemom.com), **Ovuline** (ovuline.com), & **Kindara** (kindara.com) can help you track the best time to try to conceive, track your due date once you're pregnant, help you maintain a healthy weight throughout your pregnancy, and connect you with new moms for support. It also makes predictions about when you're ovulating (most fertile) and allows users to connect with fertility experts if they have questions.

- **Baby Bump & Sprout pregnancy tracking apps** provide mothers with daily information about their specific stage of pregnancy. Baby Bump (babybumpapp.com) allows users to share info and learn from mothers at the same stage of pregnancy. Sprout can store 3-D images from your ultrasound so you can share those pictures (medart-studios.com).

- **My Pregnancy Today** provides users with daily information and advice, pertinent nutritional info, a pregnancy checklist for doctor's appointments, educational materials via images and videos, and a platform to connect with other moms who are near your due date (babycenter.com/my-pregnancy-today-app).

- **Glow** helps women conceive by providing a step-by-step guidance based on evaluating their menstrual cycle, sexual activity, body mass index, peak conception days, and other factors (glowing.com).

Baby Care

- **Trixie Tracker** (trixietracker.com) & **BabyBix** (babybix.com) help you store your baby's habits, including sleeping, feeding, and diaper changes. It allows you to keep track of newly introduced foods and manage your milk inventory. It also offers a medication management tool when your baby is ill.

Diabetes

- **WellDoc** allows diabetics to easily record glucose levels and other details about their diabetes (welldoc.com).

- **Omada Health's** program has a comprehensive 16-week program designed to help those who are at risk for Type 2 diabetes lose weight and prevent diabetes. Each person is assigned a health coach to walk them through the entire process. The goal is to help users make positive behavior changes (omadahealth.com).

There are numerous other ones that you can find online as well. I wanted to provide a few that might give you some insight into how to better manage your diabetes.

Seizures & Brain Stuff

- **Epdetect** uses the accelerometer in the phone to detect when a person has fallen and then sends a text message to a caregiver so they can respond and provide assistance (epdetect.com).

- **My Epilepsy Diary** helps you record details of what's happened during an event. It also helps track your medications and dosages and alerts you when you may have missed a dose (epilepsy.com/seizuredairy).

- **MoodTune** has used neuroscience research to develop tasks that boost your mood. If you are suffering from depression, stress, anxiety, post-partum depression, or PTSD, these simple in-app tasks have been shown to improve symptoms and lift your mood (braintracercorp.com).

- **Lumosity** offers tools to train your brain with games designed by neuroscientists to exercise your memory and attention (lumosity.com).

- **Thync** has a wearable technology that sticks to your temple then sends tiny impulses generated by the program. The impulses actively jolt the neurons in two sensitive areas of the brain that produce relaxation, and another designed to produce alertness. This type of neurosignaling generates a shift in your state of mind (thync.com).

- **Constant Therapy** was developed from research at Boston University. They can be used to speed the treatment of patients who have suffered a stroke, head injury, dementia, or other cognitive disorder (constanttherapy.com).

- **Quotient** has developed a computer program that can test for ADHD and track over time how your child is doing (quotient-adhd.com).

- **Traxion** allows young adults to manage their ADHD symptoms (traxion.me).

Asthma

- **AsthmaMD** allows users to easily and quickly log their asthma activity (severity, triggers, time/date, and location) and medications in the form of a diary. Users can share the diary and a color graph chart of their asthma activities with their physicians to be included in their medical records. They can also opt into a program that allows them to anonymously send their data to researchers, providing scientists with unprecedented insight into the causes and correlation of asthma flares (asthmamd.org).

- **AsthmaSense** allows asthmatic patients to follow symptoms, record triggers, record use of regularly scheduled meds (as needed meds) and rescue meds, record peak flow measurements, and enter wheeze rates. A tap of the Rescue button alerts your emergency contact that you're having a severe attack and will allow you to get help quickly. This company is also developing a device called AirSonea, which detects and measures wheezing (asthmasense.com).

Your Parents

- **Care4Today** helps improve medication adherence. There are more than 20,000 prescription and over-the-counter drugs pre-programmed. It includes pictures of the pills so users can set alarms and reminders that will deliver specific cues about what meds to take. This is great for people with multiple medications that need a way to ensure that they are taking the right medication. Users can print out a 7-day or 30-day report of their adherence that they can share with their doctors (care4today.com).

This chapter covers **specific conditions and only a few companies that are transforming them**. Visit my blog at healthdisrupted.com for an updated list.

Apps From The Big Players Reinvent Patient Engagement

The power of health apps has not escaped the largest players in the health ecosystem. Pharmacy chains, insurers, health systems, individual doctors, and even wireless carriers are developing their own ones and mobile health initiatives. **Apple**, for example, with its Apple Health Kit is creating a new platform for health app development, which should provide valuable tools for you.

Walgreens, CVS, and **Rite Aid** are large pharmacy chains pushing for new roles and different types of engagement with patients. All these companies offer apps that allow customers to refill medications and get prescription reminders. Some pharmacies even go beyond refills. For example, CVS allows you to check for medication interactions; identify drugs based on shape, color, and imprint; see your prescription history; and schedule your immunizations.

Helping Patients Take Their Medications

Janice is a 36-year-old mother of two who works as an interior designer. She has no major health problems, but takes birth control and thyroid medications. She marks the day she should call her pharmacy to refill her prescription on her calendar, which is a pretty good method (when she remembers to check it). She has forgotten on a couple of occasions and gone several days without taking her medications.

Then Janice discovered her pharmacy's app. It allowed her to set reminders when she needs a refill. She can scan the barcode of the prescription and send the refill request directly to the pharmacist. A few hours later, Janice has her prescription in hand.

She never imagined it could be so easy to coordinate her refills and get reminders. The convenience of this feature meant she never had to miss a pill because calling for a refill "slipped her mind."

Health insurance firms have also recognized the importance of providing mobile tools to their plan members. Many now provide ones that allow patients to find a doctor, dentist, or facility. Some review deductibles, account balances, and claims. Others check the status of claims and view personal health records. Beyond these basic offerings, some insurers (United Health, for example) provide online video chats with doctors and a nursing app that allows members to reach an RN 24/7 with medical questions. BlueCross and Aetna also offer many digital services program.

Finally, cellular providers are also actively engaged with companies to offer real time monitoring with embedded wireless connections to store and share data. All the major companies have built out healthcare teams and are actively investing and partnering in this area. Don't be surprised if you see more health offerings from cell companies. Here are a few examples:

- **AT&T's** health strategy is centered on letting their consumers manage their own health. Partnering with **WellDoc**, they allow diabetic patients to upload information like blood sugar readings and photos of wounds and submit them to their physicians for immediate review. AT&T has also co-developed a device called **Asthma Triggers**, which has a wireless sensor that scans the air and measures pollutants that could set off asthma attacks. Data from multiple customers is uploaded and tracked so that an alert can be given out when there is an uptick of asthma triggers.

- **Verizon** has developed a home monitoring platform in which biometric data, such as blood pressure, glucose measurements, and oxygen saturation levels, can be collected. This data will help clinicians send tasks, recommendations, surveys, educational materials, and motivational messages.

- **Sprint** has teamed up with **BodyMedia** to add cellular connectivity to its popular FIT Armband. Sprint has also forged a relationship with **HealthSpot**—a company that owns primary and specialty care kiosks located in pharmacies, supermarkets, and workplaces. Patients using the kiosk can visit with doctors in real time via videoconferencing.

As the adage goes, an apple a day keeps the doctor away. Well, apps truly are the new "apples" in terms of driving digital prevention. Even if you don't have any health issues, there are a number of them that can be helpful for your family or can help you meet your fitness and nutrition goals. Unfortunately, it can feel overwhelming, given the number of them that are available. This book hopes to point you in the right direction and provide a framework for you to think about when engaging with them. *Bon appetit!*

6

YOUR BLOOD CAN PREDICT YOUR FUTURE

The biggest revolution in medicine will happen inside our cells. Our blood and other cells provide the pathway for predicting disease, and therefore the ability to try to pre-empt the disease process.

Pre-emptive medicine is based on science's increasing ability to understand signals that cells emit when under attack or failing. It's also based on powerful innovations that are allowing companies to use this new scientific understanding to create products that doctors and patients can use. In essence, pre-emptive approaches will **take healthcare down a clearer, cellular path**. These tremendous new scientific developments allow us to:

1. Measure what is **happening inside the cell**
2. Understand what this means for the body
3. **Correlate this** to disease events

Historically, physicians have relied primarily on *family history and ethnicity* to place patients into various risk groups, which is often an unreliable way to predict diseases. This is why, in the same family, one brother can have diabetes while the other does not. Both have the same family history and ethnicity, but they may have different cellular context. Ultimately, it is a combination of genetics and the environment that drives the progression of diseases—and that is why examining elements in the blood can provide a more accurate assessment.

In fact, our understanding of cell biology has come a long way. We are **now better equipped to see signals emanating from cells** in the form of chemicals, proteins, and markers of inflammation. These signals tell us what is going on inside our cells. This information can be analyzed by an algorithm to alert doctors of the presence of diseases much earlier than traditional diagnostics.

Understanding what our blood is telling us is covered more fully later in the book. Needless to say, some experts argue that understanding predictive markers of disease will drive the biggest revolution in medicine.

Our blood can also help us optimize our activities. For example, **Inside Tracker** measures vitamins and nutrients in blood and provides recommendations to optimize health and athletic performance (insidetracker.com).

Moreover, this approach to medicine could help you avoid getting an expensive and cumbersome invasive test. For example, **Exact Sciences** offers a test, which can potentially replace a colonoscopy for the detection of colon cancer. Many people avoid colonoscopy and that is one reason why colon cancer rates remain steady. By making it easy to get screened through a home stool test kit, this approach should radically improve the ability to detect colon cancer early.

I will now take a deep dive into technologies that can provide better predictions. Let's discuss how you can have more information about your risk for:

1. Heart attacks
2. Diabetes
3. Scoliosis and autism (in your children)
4. Breast, oral, and lung cancer
5. At-risk pregnancy

Insider Tips

11. In the coming decades, **more conditions will be detected pre-emptively in our cells**—what's included in this book is just the tip of the iceberg.

12. **Take the lead on preventing heart attacks, diabetes, cancer, etc.** Many conditions can now be averted. Sometimes you have to pay out of pocket for these tests—and that is okay. Health insurance firms are often slow to reimburse new technologies.

Prevent Your Own Heart Attack

Consider sudden cardiac arrest, which claims almost 250,000 American lives a year.[7] Many of these deaths are preventable.

We have all heard of celebrities, relatives, and friends dying at relatively young ages in their 40's and 50's from cardiac arrest.

For example, *The Sopranos* star James Gandolfini recently died at 51, highlighting that even people with access to great medical care and the best doctors are susceptible to premature death.

Notable Individuals With Diseases That Could Have Been Detected Earlier

1. Patrick Swazye – Pancreatic Cancer – Age 57

2. Steve Jobs – Pancreatic Cancer – Age 56

3. President Bill Clinton – Multiple Vessel Heart Disease – Age 63

Innovative diagnostic companies are using blood tests to more accurately predict when you may have a heart attack. The reason this is significant is that most doctors don't currently tailor cardiac screening recommendations to your specific genetics and biology.

Doctors have outdated training and typically rely primarily on *qualitative information* such as family history and certain risk factors like smoking, high blood pressure, high cholesterol, and diabetes. They order screening tests based on this lower-quality data. Doctors do this because they were trained during a time when we did not understand the *quantitative science* that was happening at the cellular level. But traditional risk factors can only go so far in triaging patients—in pinpointing those most at risk.

This is why so many patients with no risk factors have heart attacks. In fact, a scientific paper by Khol et al., in the *Journal of the American Medical Association*, showed that among patients, who have had cardiac arrest, 62% (the majority of patients) have 0-1 risk factors, 50% have normal cholesterol levels, and 17% have no risk factors. Even shocking to me!

What this tells us is we do not know a lot about what the risk factors are when it comes to heart disease; **therefore, we cannot rely on risk factors alone**. It is incumbent on patients to learn about ways to monitor their own heart.

Predicting Heart Attacks By Peering Into Cells

CardioDx has created a screening test, called **Corus CAD**, that detects heart proteins circulating in the blood. It allows for a more objective way to classify at-risk patients. High-risk patients can receive a cardiac catheterization more promptly.

It will also help you to change your behavior. If your cells are screaming "you are at a high risk for heart disease," then it becomes much easier to avoid that Krispy Kreme donut (cardiodx.com).

Get A 5-Year Weather Forecast For Diabetes

Diabetes is a deadly chronic disease in dire need of pre-emptive strategies. Genetics alone is not a good predictor of who will get diabetes. What if you knew you were at risk of developing diabetes in the next five years? Would you proactively change your eating, exercise, and weight management habits to reduce and potentially eradicate that risk? New technologies can help you do just that:

- **Tethys Bioscience** created a simple test that measures proteins in the blood to help doctors more accurately predict if a particular patient will get Type 2 diabetes within the next five years. Unfortunately, Tethys has closed, but there is some hope that their technology will re-emerge.

- **Prognomix** is a company with four tests in development that uses genomic signatures to predict and pre-empt diabetes (prognomix.com).

Shaping Your Diabetes Destiny

Jack is a 40-year-old software developer. After seeing his parents plagued by diabetes, he became more concerned about his own risks. He is lean and dogmatically watches what he eats. Unfortunately for him, he likes cookies and cakes. He sees his doctor and finds out that his blood sugar is a little elevated, which places Jack in the pre-diabetic category. *What does this mean?* he wonders. *Am I doomed to get diabetes after all?*

Jack searches "pre-diabetes" and finds a test called PreDx. On their website he reads that this test measures seven proteins in the blood to accurately predict the risk of diabetes within the next five years. Through his physician, Jack arranges to get the PreDx test done. He gets his results in a week. His score is 5, which is intermediate risk. He is relieved and feels more hopeful that he can avert diabetes completely, so he cuts sweets out of his diet. A year later he takes the test again. His results are even better—his score is a 3, which is low risk. He feels relieved and empowered: *I was actually able to change my diabetes destiny*, he thinks.

Make Your Kids Take A Different Type Of Test

Chances are, 1 in 3 people reading this book will have some form of scoliosis (a curvature of the spine). However, some forms of scoliosis can be severely debilitating. Currently, pediatricians use X-rays to examine the degree of spine curvature, but X-rays can't predict who will develop severe disease. Knowing this information ahead of time will allow for early intervention with spine braces, and circumvent the need for much more invasive and risky spine surgeries later.

Axial Biotech was able to identify a set of genes that correlate to scoliosis. Their genetic test, called the ScoliScore, is significantly better than X-rays for determining which patients are prone to developing severe scoliosis. In fact, the test has a 90% accuracy rate in predicting if a patient will get a severe form of scoliosis (scoliscore.com). **Transgenomic** has acquired Axial's technology.

By predicting which kids are at high risk for developing a severe form of the disease, spine surgeons can then initiate interventions sooner and eliminate the need for major spine surgery for some children. The other benefit of using this test is that pediatricians will be able to order fewer X-rays and reduce children's radiation exposure. Another test that might be a little bit more controversial but no less important is in the area of autism. As most people know, autism is a condition of high medical and emotional costs. Some believe that by diagnosing earlier, there's hope that starting interventions sooner will lead to improved outcomes for children. **SynapDx** is developing a blood test that can screen for autism earlier than traditional screening. The technology is still in early development, but worth following (synapdx.com).

Again, I am placing these examples here not to indicate that everyone should get screened for all disorders, but merely to show you that there are tests that could be helpful for some families.

Screening For Cancer Risks, Like Celebrities

Angelina Jolie very notably chose to be screened for breast cancer using the **BRCA test**, which identifies genetic markers that indicate a high risk of developing breast and ovarian cancer. Her results were significant—87% increased risk for cancer. So at 38 she preemptively decided to get a double mastectomy.

Genetic testing can be expensive, ranging from $300 to $5,000. There is also controversy on whether insurance firms should cover this test. But over time there will be lower-cost versions of the test from new competitors like laboratory companies **Quest** and **Labcorp** that will make it more accessible for women who want to get tested.

For those who want a more in-depth overview of cancer science and diagnostics, there is a very informative **PBS** television series called *Cancer: Emperor of All Maladies*, based on the book with the same name by Siddhartha Mukherjee. Watch the movie for free on PBS.org.

Numerous companies are developing cancer screening tests:

- **Exact Sciences** has developed Cologuard which recognizes the DNA generated from shedding colon cancer cells found in the stool. The company reports in a clinical study of Cologuard, that 92% of cancers and 69% of precancerous cells were identified. The test is performed at home which is much less invasive than a colonoscopy (exactsciences.com).

- **Myriad Genetics** developed the BRCA test to help determine the likelihood of developing breast cancer or ovarian cancer. For patients who have a hereditary predisposition, this test will identify if there are mutations in the BRCA region of a person's DNA corresponding with increased risk. Women with this mutation have an increased risk of developing breast cancer (up to 87%) and ovarian cancer (up to 44%) by age 70 (myriad.com).

- **Mira Dx** offers a screening test for breast and ovarian cancer using a different gene mutation called KRAS. This is a different DNA marker that is found in the blood and will likely complement the BRCA test (miradx.com).

Oral Cancer Detection Before It's Visible

Identifying oral cancer early is extremely important because surgeries for treating these cancers can be disfiguring. Imagine if you could prevent having part of your jaw removed!

The problem is that the primary way cancers are detected is by visually inspecting the mouth. It is really difficult for you or me to fully examine our mouths by ourselves. However, by the time dentists notice a suspicious lesion, it often requires invasive, potentially disfiguring surgery as treatment.

For example, **Zila** (which was acquired by DenMat) offers a test called **Vizilite** to detect oral cancer well ahead of what a physician or dentist could see just by visually examining. Providers coat the mouth with a special dye and then use the Vizilite device to identify oral cells that may be prone to becoming cancerous. These cells can then be biopsied and treatment can start earlier, hopefully enabling you to avoid surgery (denmat.com/TBlue).

Detecting Lung Cancer Before X-rays

Lung cancer is another disease that has troubled doctors because of the lack of screening tools that can catch harmful changes earlier. Traditional detection methods rely on imaging and subsequent biopsy of the suspicious tissue—which is difficult and high risk; and detects cancers at later stages.

However, lung cells can reveal early signs of cancer that manifest inside the DNA and protein of these cells. Until recently, there was little progress in diagnostic tests that could differentiate between healthy airway cells and ones that were cancerous. But early detection tests have the capacity to enable early diagnosis and, importantly, can lead to precise treatment of lung cancer and other lung diseases.

Below are a few innovative companies making a difference in cancer detection:

- **Oncimmune** (acquired by Health Diagnostics Laboratory) has developed a test called Early CDT that uses protein markers in the blood to detect lung cancer as much as **five years ahead of a chest X-ray** (earlycdt-lung.co.uk).

- **Allegro Diagnostics** (acquired by Veracyte) has developed a test that determines your risk for lung cancer by comparing the information coming from healthy and unhealthy lung cells through genomic analysis (veracyte.com).

If you were in a position where you or someone you love was at risk for one of these cancers, wouldn't you want to know about these screening technologies? Being a Smart Patient means *bringing up conversations about innovative cancer screening tests with your physician.* I am hoping to make more people aware of these lifesaving advances.

Making At-Risk Pregnancies Safer

A number of companies are helping to make pregnancies safer, thus reducing parental anxiety. Advances in science have allowed us to identify and isolate cells from the baby that circulate in the mom's bloodstream. Scientists have figured out that some of the fragments of a fetus's DNA circulate in their mothers and can be detected as early as seven weeks. The DNA comes from fetal cells that mix in the placenta. These fragments are isolated and analyzed using traditional genetic tools.

The main benefit is that physicians and parents can use a simple blood test to tell if the baby has genetic issues without having to do an amniocentesis, a procedure performed by inserting a needle into the womb to extract fetal cells. Amniocentesis can only be done much later in the pregnancy (about 16 weeks) and has potential for complications such as infection and premature labor.

For example, **Verinata** (acquired by Illumina) has developed a prenatal test—done by a simple blood draw from the mother—that screens for Down syndrome, Edwards syndrome, Patau syndrome, and sex chromosomes. Also, it allows for parents to know the gender earlier. Again controversial, but it might be helpful for some (illumina.com). **Natera** has developed a similar test (natera.com).

There are also tests that can help mothers become healthier before pregnancy. Women have all heard that you need to take folate before pregnancy to prevent spina bifida. Normally you need to start taking folate eight weeks prior to conception, but most women wait until they are pregnant before they start taking it (in prenatal vitamins). Moreover, scientists have figured that genetically only some women need to do this. **VitaPath Genetics** (bought by Alere) has created a genetic test to determine whether a woman **will need folate supplementation during pregnancy** to prevent birth defects. By identifying mothers who actually need folate—based on their biochemistry—doctors can provide the right dose of folate and prevent spina bifida in the baby. For women who are trying to conceive, this genetic test could be beneficial ahead of conception (alere.com).

Do-It-Yourself Care—Home Diagnostics
I have added this section to highlight the increasing interest by consumers to get tests that they can do on their own without having

to see a doctor first. In fact, not long ago, patients saw doctors at clinics and hospitals to get simple blood glucose measurements and even pregnancy tests.

Also, many of these tests can be ordered online, highlighting how we now live in the digital era of medicine. Imagine if you could diagnose yourself with a urinary tract infection (UTI) at home with a kit rather than making a trip to the doctor's office. The results could be emailed directly to you or scanned and sent to the doctor. They would call in a prescription for you without requiring you to endure an in person visit. Or imagine if your child had a cough, runny nose, or perhaps a fever. You could use an at-home flu-screening kit to check whether they should be kept home from school.

Some companies are developing at-home testing kits:

- **Home Access** offers HIV, hepatitis C, and cholesterol home tests, among others. You collect a small blood sample with the kit and mail it back. Results are available within a week (homeaccess.com).

- **MyAllergyTest** is a home blood test for the 10 most common allergens. You buy the kit and send it back with a collected blood sample. Results of what you are allergic to are then available online; they also offer clinical support and referrals to other products and resources (immunetech.com).

Diagnosing HIV At Home

According to the Centers for Disease Control (CDC), more than one million people in the United States are infected with HIV. In fact, the CDC estimates that **20% of people who have HIV do not know they are infected.** A diagnostic company,

Orasure, has developed the first FDA-approved home test kit for HIV, allowing patients to discreetly test themselves in just minutes whenever and wherever they want. The convenience of an at-home HIV testing makes it attractive.

The HIV test kit uses oral swabs to determine HIV status in 15 minutes. This at-home screening tool targets high-risk patients: many who don't have access to healthcare. The immediacy of the results and the convenience of an at home test could further increase the percentage of people getting tested. Getting tested *and* receiving the results quickly is vital to decreasing the number of new cases each year (oraquick.com).

Identifying signals in our blood (and other body fluids) will be a cornerstone for future therapies and catching disease earlier in its tracks. Although some companies may be sold or shutdown, it is **helpful for you to keep connected to the research and the startups that are leading the way** in this exciting area of medicine.

As I mentioned in the digital game plan, you need to think of health investments in both the short-term and long-term. Screening yourself for potential issues and knowing your risks goes a long way toward long-term planning. The next step is to take the lead on staying up-to-date and one way to do this is to think of yourself as a student of health and train with Dr. Google.

7

TRAIN WITH DOCTOR GOOGLE

T he Internet has become the biggest medical repository ever created. With clinical research articles and Wikipedia, nearly every conceivable medical question now has a "Googleable" answer. It has become the *de facto* place to start searching for health information for most people. According to The Pew Center, 80% of US adults look up health information online. Given this revolution in access to medical information, I believe the time is now to have patients become much better versed in **medical terminology** and **medical decision making.** As mentioned, we need to close the medical literacy gap if we want to truly lower healthcare costs.

Although many of us find information online to be either too generic or too scientific. This chapter demonstrates how to streamline the training process and avoid websites that have erroneous information. Over time, I believe, websites with misleading information will be weeded out.

I am going to show how each of you can become true partners; so the next time you see your doctor, you can be prepared to have an interactive conversation. In fact, numerous health systems like the Mayo Clinic and digital startups are creating an anchor point for health information. Mayo and Google have recently announced (in 2015) that they are partnering to show health related online search results that have passed the Mayo Clinic review. Imagine **"Mayo Reviewed"** next to the search results when you type in "what causes heart disease."

This should go a long way to **making training on the Internet a sound and safe investment.** Of course, this does not mean I am suggesting you should try to treat Uncle Frank's illness from what you learn online!

From Your Public Library

The Library Association of America profiles trusted health websites broken down by categories such as senior health and parenting at caphis.mlanet.org.

To become a great partner for your doctor, you will need to cover a few basic topics so you can learn the language of medicine, disease basics, diagnosis, and treatment. Fortunately, companies are creating medical databases that take medical research and translate them into language patients can understand. They're making these "translations" readily available on the Internet.

Here is a breakdown of topics that are often covered in medical school and that you could (or should) get instruction in:

1. Basic anatomy & medical terminology
2. Diseases

3. Treatments
4. Drug interactions
5. Nutrition
6. Q&A with doctors

I have reviewed numerous online learning resources and have highlighted a few below that can provide a jump-start. In fact, some physicians, medical students, and healthcare workers will find these resources helpful to keep up-to-date with current medical practices.

Insider Tips

13. **Prepare for your next doctor's appointment.** You can actually learn a lot online. Develop a list of questions. Then check your favorite health websites and take notes to discuss with your doctor.

14. **After your doctor's visit, research their recommendations.** If your doctor says you have high blood pressure, read about its impact on the body and what you can do about it.

To illustrate this, let's walk through the process by using Mark, a 53-year-old project manager who wants to become a co-pilot in his medical care. To do so, he needs a basic understanding and knowledge of the following:

1. **Basic anatomy & medical terminology**

   To start, Mark goes to **InnerBody.com** where he sees a map of all the parts of the body. Mark has a bad knee, and he wants to talk to his doctor about it. He is able to see pictures of a healthy and damaged knee and gets familiar with the names of different parts. After his doctor's visit he is able to visualize what the doctor is saying and sees what a meniscus tear is, for example.

Another option for Mark to learn the basics is by visiting the largest medical image library at **A.D.A.M.**, where he can also see some great pictures (adamimages.com). Mark can also access the **University of Iowa's** database, which lists great resources to learn about his bad knee (hardinmd. lib.uiowa.edu). He double clicks on *Skeletal* and *Knee Pain*, and is given a list of top health resources to get more information.

Mark's doctor could also use **Orca Health,** which lets his doctor create personalized images and recommendations by writing on top of the image. They also offer medical education by offering movie-quality educational materials. Mark can learn in real time on his smartphone or device by touching, hearing, and seeing information about his knee—much better than a brochure.

2. **Diseases**

Mark has asthma and has never understood why his symptoms seem to come and go. He tries to avoid smoke and pollen, but sometimes his asthma flares up for no reason. Mark decides to go to **HealthGuru.com**, a website with one of the largest libraries of health videos on the Internet. They provide the basic information needed for a broad understanding of various topics.

To supplement the information he found on HealthGuru, Mark also went to **HealthiNation.com**, which offers TV-style professional videos of physicians explaining certain disease processes and answering health related questions.

Mark found a few videos that helped him with his asthma—they were also entertaining to watch.

He also checks out a site that his family doctor uses called **Familydoctor.org**, which provides health information for all educational backgrounds.

3. **Treatments**

Mark finds some information on his knee and asthma at **FoundHealth.com**, which details treatment options and provides a holistic approach to recommendations, paired with feedback from real patients who have used these therapies.

Because Mark is in his 50s, he gets targeted for a lot of men's health issues. He notices that every time he watches CNN there is an ad for low testosterone (low T) treatment. The ads say that if he's having low energy and low libido, he should think about low T treatment. Mark is experiencing both low energy and low libido, but he is a little suspicious and wants to get some facts and understand what the clinical evidence is for treating low T.

To learn more about treatment options, Mark tries a few websites, including **EverdayHealth.com**, **WebMD.com**, and **Health.com**. He was able to cross-reference the three sites and figure out treatment options.

4. **Drug interactions**

Mark also wanted to get more information on his asthma medications and potential side effects with testosterone supplementation. He found **MediGuard. com**, which is designed to help patients learn more about their medications and closely monitor what they take. The website covers how drugs interact with each other. He sets up an email alert to receive safety information about specific medications as well as get feedback from the website members on similar medications.

Mark also looked up the medications his 78-year-old mother takes on **Medwatcher.org,** which was created in collaboration with the Food and Drug Administration (FDA) to monitor side effects of drugs.

Given the growing number of drugs that patients are currently taking (on average four drugs after age 60), drug safety will be an important aspect of taking care of your health or your aging parent's health.

5. **Nutrition**

Mark is a fitness nut, watches what he eats, and is eager to learn more about improving his overall health.

He began his research by downloading **Fooducate,** which provides detailed nutritional information by scanning an item's barcode. While using Fooducate in a grocery store, he felt like he was taking a crash course on nutrition because he learned so much (fooducate.com).

Mark likes to read about alternative therapies and enjoys wellness articles. He went to **Greatist.com,** where he found a lengthy list of wellness articles with great visuals.

6. **Q&A with doctors**

An important aspect of getting trained is the ability to directly interact with doctors and ask questions. There are a number of online resources where you can do just that.

Mark tried **HealthTap.com,** which allows patients to ask doctors questions online or on their smartphones. HealthTap has a database of thousands of questions that have already been answered by doctors. Mark typed "low testosterone" and found hundreds of questions from patients, including the real answers from doctors.

The "training with Dr. Google" approach doesn't cover all the topics you would learn in medical school, but believe me, the majority of what you need to know can be found online and in a format that you can understand. You don't need, or likely want, to take a class on organic chemistry or microbiology to become a great partner for your doctor.

There are a large number of health portals that provide wonderful information and this list of online resources keeps growing.

Below are a few select sources from highly reputable organizations:

- **General Health** – Aetna's Intelihealth sources information from Harvard and Columbia, so it is state of the art (intelihealth.com).

- **Women's Health** – womenshealthresources.nlm.nih.gov sources the National Institute of Health.

- **Men's Health** – for men interested in men's sexual and urinary health, visit urologyhealth.org.

- **Children's Health** – for information from one of the top hospitals, the Hospital for Sick Children – aboutkidshealth. ca.

- **Mental Health for Children** – a great place to start researching children's mental health issues – aacap.org.

- **Caregivers Support** – caregiver.org provides information and support in multiple languages, including English, Spanish, Chinese, Korean, Vietnamese, and others.

- **Herbal and Vitamin Supplements** – try longwoodherbal. org for great information on herbal medicine, dietary supplements, and vitamins for both consumers and professionals.

Select List Of Health Education Portals

Health.com

HealthCentral.com

Healthetreatment.com

Healthline.com

ChickRx.com

Institute of Medicine (iom.edu)

Mayo Clinic (mayoclinic.org)

MedHelp.org

National Institutes of Health (nih.gov)

ShareCare.com

WebMD.com

Wellsphere.com

In this chapter, I am trying to show you that you can learn medical materials in a relatively quick manner. Moreover, the Internet is still early in its evolution. I imagine that health education content will only continue to get better. There will be an increasing number of tools to enable you to become a great co-pilot in your care.

To continue down the path of digital prevention, the next chapter discusses how novel devices can be used to help set up a physical surveillance program for your body. It is a completely different way of thinking about how we can manage our health and identify serious medical conditions before they happen.

8

ADD AN ALARM SYSTEM TO YOUR BODY

W hat if you could have a device protect your health like an ADT security system that watches over your home? What if this was possible for your older parents or a pregnant spouse? You may have heard that Google has developed a contact lens that can sense low or high blood sugar and alerts patients with diabetic issues. Imagine not having to prick your finger multiple times a day but continuously being monitored. This is the power of adding an alarm system to your body.

Medical devices are getting smarter and more user-friendly. These convenient, easy-to-use gadgets are able to pick up signals from the body and translate them in a way that can notify you of an impending health issue. Smart Patients will know how to interact and ask for these new technologies.

According to iData Research, health monitoring is a $3.1 billion market in the US. It's expected to grow by 25% in the next five years, with its growth primarily driven by the ability to monitor patients outside the hospital.

Below we explore these new "alarm systems" to give you a flavor of the innovation happening right now. I hope the examples will paint an exciting picture of how healthcare is being transformed. Learn how these devices can make:

1. Baby monitoring better
2. Heart monitoring easier
3. Seizures safer
4. Asthma flare-ups fewer

Insider Tips

15. **Consider heart rhythm monitoring as you get older.** Monitoring yourself every few years can be a valuable way to detect heart problems and factors that can lead to stroke.

16. **Share novel monitoring technologies with your doctor.** Some of these monitoring devices are still new and your doctor may not have heard about them.

"Baby Bump" Gets Smart

Pregnancy can create a significant stress on the body, and in some cases on the baby, without obvious symptoms. A number of different technologies are being developed to help improve and detect conditions within the fetus earlier and also detect any other potential issues arising from pregnancy.

One way to determine fetal stress is to monitor the baby's heart rate. A significantly low or high heart rate can indicate that the fetus is experiencing low oxygen, infections, and/or bleeding within the uterus. This monitoring often requires mothers to spend hours at the hospital. In some parts of the US and many parts of the world, getting to a hospital to get monitored can be problematic.

Sense4Baby (acquired by Airstrip) has developed a simple, convenient way to monitor at-risk pregnant women at home by continuously analyzing their baby's heart rate through a wireless monitor, which is worn across the abdomen. The data is transmitted to the doctor for monitoring (airstrip.com).

This helps with an important issue: the fact that the fetus may be in distress without obvious signs. Real time monitoring allows for early detection and immediate intervention, which can improve pregnancy outcomes for mom and baby.

Heart Rhythm Monitors Can Pre-empt Cardiac Arrests & Strokes

About half of all cardiac arrests occur in patients **who don't know they have abnormal heart rhythms.** This phenomenon is called *sudden cardiac arrest*, when the heart stops beating effectively and fails to pump blood, resulting in death. Abnormal heart rhythms are also one of the main reasons people have strokes. This particular arrhythmia is known as atrial fibrillation—when the top chambers of the heart beat irregularly, allowing blood to pool and clots to form. These clots can become dislodged and travel to the brain, causing a stroke.

Increasing the use of cardiac monitoring devices should help identify those patients at risk for both sudden cardiac arrest and stroke. For example, if a patient's heart rhythm becomes fatally fast (a disorder known as ventricular tachycardia), then this patient can get a defibrillator, which can prevent sudden cardiac arrest.

iRhythm has developed the Zio Patch, which is the size of a Band-Aid and enables the wearer to monitor their heart without wearing bulky, cumbersome devices with tangle prone wires (irhythmtech.com). The patch sends data to the doctor that can help the doctor determine:

1. if the rhythm is harmful, and
2. if it occurs frequently enough to warrant intervention

The beauty of this type of monitoring device is that it can pre-emptively determine whether a patient needs a cardiac intervention. If atrial fibrillation is found (irregular heartbeat), patients can begin taking medications to prevent clots that can cause strokes, or a defibrillator if they have ventricular tachycardia.

Most people who have strokes don't physically know that they have an irregular heartbeat, because it can come and go over a day or week. Therefore, it is important to monitor the heart rhythm for at least 1 to 2 weeks to pick up infrequent irregular beats.

The Zio Patch addresses one of the biggest issues that plagues traditional monitoring—*patient compliance*. The old standard method requires the patient to wear 12 wires and a large cellphone shaped device known as a Holter monitor, which most patients find too cumbersome to wear.

The small size of the Zio Patch also allows for a high compliance rate with patients, meaning they will actually wear it. Since it is easier to wear, a patient will wear it longer—up to two weeks. With more data, physicians get a much better analysis to identify abnormal heart rhythms. Digital monitoring technologies, therefore, are **really helping us become more compliant patients**.

Another device designed by **Corventis** also provides a similar monitoring capability; this company was bought by medical giant Medtronic (corventis.com).

Making Seizures Safer

Most patients who have seizures are never sure when one may occur, and that creates a great deal of uncertainty and anxiety in daily life. Fifty million people in the world suffer from this disorder.

But advancements in technology that allow early detection of seizures are on the horizon. This technology will alert the patient so they can find a safe place to have the seizure or notify caregivers that a seizure is imminent.

Seizures, also known as epilepsy, occur when the electrical currents in the brain go through a pattern that doesn't support normal brain function. Before a patient has a seizure, however, the brain's electrical current starts to develop an abnormal pattern (pre-seizure) that can be analyzed and distinguished from normal.

NeuroVista is developing an implantable medical device, iEEG, which allows the brain's electrical activity to be monitored continuously. As mentioned above, the brain will often have some abnormal electrical activity before a seizure occurs. These early warning signals can be detected by the iEEG, creating a pre-emptive warning so the patient can sit down or get to safety before a seizure occurs. In the past, patients would have to go to a hospital or clinic to get brain wave mapping.

Clinical studies have conclusively shown that the iEEG is able to accurately predict when a seizure will happen. Though the seizure may occur within minutes or hours, the device addresses the most debilitating part of seizures: *being unprepared*. The iEEG provides users a better and safer chance at living a more normal life (neurovista.com).

Even better than simply receiving warning of an impending seizure, new technologies are emerging that can stop a seizure entirely. **Neuropace** has developed an implantable neurostimulator that detects abnormal brain activity and responds by delivering electrical stimulation to normalize brain activity before seizure symptoms occur (neuropace.com).

An interesting wearable device, the **SmartWatch**, is a wristwatch that detects movement outside the normal spectrum and instantly alerts caregivers via their phones. It automatically collects key data during any seizure episodes. This will help with getting help sooner and is a relatively inexpensive and easy-to-use product (smart-monitor.com).

Making Asthma Management Less Unpredictable

Millions of Americans suffer from asthma and many of them are children. One of the critical issues with asthma is the unpredictable nature of the disease. There are numerous triggers such as going for a run outside in the fall, a visiting friend who has dog hair on his jacket, or increased smog coming from a neighboring city.

In fact, asthma patients have a number of jobs they must do each day to manage their asthma:

1. Take inhaler medications daily
2. Avoid environmental triggers
3. Monitor symptoms such as wheezing or shortness of breath

Given the number of daily and repetitive jobs, asthma patients often don't comply with the treatment programs that their doctors recommend. This can lead to asthma flares and increased visits to the doctor's office and ER. Given the daily hassle, asthma management is a great area for digital health to create an impact.

As mentioned, a number of apps (like AsthmaMD and AsthmaSense) have been developed to provide information like pollen count and barometric pressure, which are two main triggers. Startups are also tackling the traditional method to determine how your lungs are doing—peak flow meter testing. You blow into the meter and it tells you the maximal flow. **Cohero Health** and **MySpiroo** have developed meters (peak flow) that you can breathe into to assess if you are having an early sign of a flare, and then guide you to take the right action. By starting therapy early in the course of an asthma flare, it can significantly decrease the likelihood of an ER visit or hospitalization (coherohealth.com, myspiroo.com).

Another innovative company, **Propeller Health**, has created a device that can attach to an inhaler to monitor its proper usage. It is especially good for parents to follow their children's usage, or if you forget to use your inhaler, it can remind you (propellerhealth. com).

Wearables: Clothes And Cars Can Now Save Your Life

Most of us have electronics woven into our lives. We carry phones everywhere and "talk" to our cars to change the radio station. This convergence is also happening with medical monitoring into various parts of our daily lives—which is another way to add an alarm.

One notable example is a specialized shoe insert designed by **Orpyx** that can prevent foot ulcers commonly associated with diabetes. Many individuals with diabetes lose feeling in their feet and can't feel when an ulcer is forming. This is important because for many older diabetics it is physically difficult to examine their own feet.

Using pressure-sensing technology, Orpyx's shoe insert can detect the early stages of an ulcer. The information is transmitted to a watch that collects data, analyzes it, and then provides an easy interface notifying patients of impending issues (orpyx.com).

Sensors With Benefits

Low-cost sensors, smaller and smarter microchips, and better fabric technology have led to the integration of medical devices into many commonly used products.

As mentioned, Google is launching a contact lens that can measure your glucose and tell you if it is too high or too low. It can connect with a smartphone to alert users. Because it measures glucose in your tears, it can do hundreds of measurements a minute. Normally, diabetics have to prick their finger, which is painful and time-consuming and a big reason why patients avoid checking their blood sugar.

Scanadu is working to create a home diagnostic testing device—a development akin to a thermometer for the 21st century or a Star Trek-type tricorder. The device will monitor six vitals: pulse transit time, heart rate, electrical heart activity, temperature, heart rate variability, and pulse oximetry (scanadu.com).

Also, **MC10** is creating a tattoo-like sensor called the Biostamp. It can be applied to the skin and monitors body temperature, heart rate, brain activity, exposure to ultraviolet radiation, and hydration. It even alerts you when it's time to reapply sunscreen (mc10inc.com).

Another company, **Proteus**, is creating digital pills (pills that have sensors) that can communicate with a smartphone, which will help you to know if your elderly mother is taking her medications or not. It will also potentially help with optimizing the dose and minimizing side effects of medications that you may need to take, thus creating more safety when taking prescription medications (proteus.com).

As mentioned, **Smart Monitor** has created SmartWatch, a device that can detect falls with its built-in accelerometer, indicating to caregivers that an epileptic patient or elderly person has fallen (smart-monitor.com).

Car companies are integrating monitoring devices to check your blood sugar or to see if your heart is going through an abnormal rhythm. For example, **Ford** announced its partnership with **Medtronic** and **WellDoc** to integrate diabetes and asthma management applications in the car. Built-in programs will monitor drivers with diabetes or asthma, with the hopes of pre-empting episodes of low blood sugar or asthma attacks that could impair or distract drivers.

A Daily Fitness Alarm

You may have heard of (or own) a fitness tracker, and although they typically don't have alarms, they are a great way to follow your activity level and sleep. You can set alarms and reminders on most of them, which can send you a message to get up and take a walk. In fact, clinical studies show that a daily reminder to get up and exercise can be one of the most important things you can do to improve your health. ABI Research estimates that in five years the number of wearable wireless health and fitness devices will reach almost 170 million.[8]

Many trackers measure the same parameters and are differentiated primarily by ease of use, price, and size. There are too many fitness trackers to list, but below are a few to consider:

- **Fitbit, Fitbug,** and **Up by Jawbone** are wireless enabled devices that can help you monitor your exercise. They keep track of every step you take, calories burned, and you can even use them to follow sleep patterns, and weight (fitbit. com, fitbug.com, jawbone.com).

- **Misfit Wearables** has created a new fashion phenomenon by combining fitness and sleep monitoring with high-end jewelry. They want their devices to be easily integrated into your sense of style (misfit.com).

- **NikeFuel** measures movement and activity, and then allows users to utilize their online network to post and share data with their friends (nikeplus.nike.com).

- **Basis** is a digital watch with sensors that can monitor heart rate, skin temperature, and steps taken, as well as monitor sleep (mybasis.com).

- **BodyMedia** (acquired by Jawbone) is a wearable sensor that measures skin temperature, heat change, and galvanic skin response to measure how much you are sweating. It also has a built-in accelerometer. Together, these features allow for accurate measurement of calories burned and help wearers stay accountable with their fitness goals and healthy eating plans (bodymedia.com).

In this chapter, we discussed the importance of changing our mindset to one that **involves active monitoring of our medical conditions.** Now that we have explored early warning systems to help us foresee issues, let's focus on technologies that can enhance perhaps our most important asset—our brain!

9

UPGRADE YOUR BRAIN

The brain will be the next upgradeable part of the human body—and this will largely be enabled by digital health tools. By upgradeable, I mean that we will have greater **ability to modify and repair the brain's performance** with tools that will run on our phones or computers. New technologies can now identify signals in the brain that can be early indicators of disease or demonstrate how the brain is functioning after a disease has set in. This is also an emerging area of medicine called **digital therapeutics**—in which a technology can prevent or minimize a medical condition.

As we age, we increasingly rely on the brain, so small changes in brain function can have an enormous impact on how we are able to function and engage in our daily activities. The most striking age-related cognitive function that changes is memory— *where did I put my keys?* In fact, until recently neurologists affirmed that when a brain cell dies, it would not be replaced by the body. But scientists now know that brain training can clinically improve brain function. So training your brain will be as critical as working out at the gym.

The brain has been described as having **both hardware and software, similar to a computer**. The CPU, the hard drive, and memory modules are the hardware. The operating system and applications are the software that makes the hardware usable. The brain functions in a similar way—**we have our own software that allows us to see, think, hear, move, etc.** If you suffer from memory loss or poor memory recall, depression, racing thoughts, or difficulty sleeping, then these could all be symptoms of a software issue in the brain.

In the past, doctors mainly focused on problems with hardware such as in the case of a stroke to check if brain cells are damaged through an MRI. Doctors would then wait to see how much function returned. Now, doctors are using medical technologies like PET-MRI and brain mapping with electrodes worn on the head that show the intensity of cell activity, a marker for cell function.

For example, brain mapping uses *evoked potentials* (electrical signals of the brain), which measure the location and energy of brain resources. This information allows us to measure underlying brain dysfunction even when no behavioral abnormalities are apparent. Research has shown how mapping evoked potentials across the brain can determine the nature and location of brain dysfunction as well as follow treatment success during clinical care. In fact, mapping will show signs of dysfunction much earlier than even obvious signs or symptoms.

The ability to manage the software of the brain is an important area of digital health. New technologies that you can wear on your head and ones you can now use to train your brain provide us with much greater precision and direction. A number of these elements were showcased at the **Digital Health Summit** at the **Consumer Electronics Show**. The summit highlighted how the tech industry is poised to get consumers front and center in managing their own health.

Insider Tips

17. **"Working out" your brain will become an important part of your long-term health.** Science has shown that brain function can improve with training—similar to working out a muscle.

18. **Digital technologies can improve specific neurologic conditions.** The use of technology to impact these disorders has been studied over the past few decades and will likely become mainstream in the near future.

If you have children, you might be interested in learning whether your child has learning disabilities or ADHD. In diagnosing these conditions, doctors have traditionally used questionnaires and screening tools to help identify these issues. Now, in-home devices and apps can help diagnose, monitor, and even provide therapies for these conditions.

By looking at the software of the brain, we will be able to identify conditions like Alzheimer's, learning disabilities, ADHD, and others listed below:

1. Anxiety
2. Memory
3. Injury/concussion
4. Sleep disorders
5. Autism
6. Depression
7. Dementia
8. PTSD

Here are some companies that are changing the way we will manage our brains:

- **Evoke Neuroscience** is a company that has proprietary software to analyze the key performance metrics of the brain to identify issues with mental performance, memory, and sleep, using electrodes worn as a cap (evokeneuroscience.com).

- **Muse** has a brain-sensing headband that helps you to calm the mind by offering biofeedback so you can lower stress and also enter a state of meditation more quickly (choosemuse.com).

- **BrainMD** has brain-mapping technology that can show areas of high activity, which can be helpful in diagnosing issues with focus, memory, energy, and sleep. They are working with world-renowned Dr. Daniel Amen and accessing his database of over 100,000 brain scans to compare your own scan to (brainmd.com).

- **C8 Sciences** has training programs to strengthen a child's neurocognitive functions by combining computer and physical exercises to help children with ADHD, autism, and other learning disorders (c8sciences.com).

- **Neurosky** offers both heart and brain sensors that have applications in wellness similar to other companies noted (neurosky.com).

- **Quotient** has developed a computer program that can test for ADHD and follows how your child is doing over time (quotient-adhd.com).

- **Traxion** allows young adults to get better focused and manage their ADHD symptoms (traxion.me).

- **Neumitra** has a biowatch that can measure stress on the nervous system (neumitra.com).

- **Lumosity** allows users to play brain games that test memory, attention, speed, flexibility, and problem solving. Users can choose which areas of brain health they'd like to improve, and it allows you to follow your progress over time. It has been clinically shown to enhance memory in several different areas (lumosity.com).

- **Dakim** has developed "brain fitness" software that allows users to test memory by playing games. The software has been proven to produce significant improvements in memory (both immediate and delayed), language abilities, attention, focus, and concentration (dakim.com).

Over the next few years, more companies will be getting into the brain space, which will create unique opportunities for you to help yourself. The brain is vital to everything we do and is increasingly relied upon as we age. By making yourself aware of these products and technologies, it will help you to shape how your brain functions. This is also a great way to use digital technology to prevent or minimize the aging process.

10

"GOOGLE MAP" YOUR DNA

Your DNA holds a genetic blueprint that is used to build every cell of your body. As many of you know, within the DNA are genes that control various aspects of our bodies, including eye color, height, and predisposition for certain diseases. So your DNA is also a roadmap—that, to a certain degree, you can Google Map. You can identify genes, and the proteins they make, that may cause you harm down the road.

In one of the biggest breakthroughs in medicine, about 10 years ago, the human genome (the entirety of human DNA) was catalogued, and each strand of DNA was looked at and broken down into its components. It gave us a holistic view of the entire set of programs that are used to run the cells in our bodies.

Today, in an international effort, the DNA of millions of patients is being **catalogued along with any diseases** they may have. This allows scientists to determine which genes are correlated with certain diseases. Out of an estimated 20,000 to 25,000 genes, 3,669 of them are currently known to be associated with diseases.[9]

Another important development is **the ability for anyone to get genetic testing at a reasonably low cost.** This digital innovation inside these gene-deciphering instruments is the reason why the prices have come down. When gene analysis first came out, it was expensive ($50,000) and we couldn't do much with the information. Over a short period of time, seven years, the price has dropped below $1,000. As the price lowers (with improved technology), then it is more likely that everyday folks will be able to get their genetic readout.

Since your genetic code can be easily read, the next step is to know what to do if you possess a variant of a gene. If you have a variant, does it mean you will definitely get that disease? It depends: we know that environmental factors play a significant role in determining who gets a condition—or at least provide a relative risk of developing one. But I think having this information would put a lot more control in your hands. If you know you are *predisposed to lung cancer or asthma*, wouldn't that deter you from smoking or living in high-pollen areas respectively? Or if you knew that you were *predisposed to skin cancer*, would you be better at remembering to wear sunscreen? These diagnostic screening tools put the onus on the patient to take action. This can be scary, but there are people trained to help you analyze this information.

The field of genetic counseling, which translates genetic information into actionable steps for the patient, is rapidly expanding. This field of medicine is so new that most doctors don't yet have a handle on when to offer DNA genotyping for their patients. This may change soon. But it is important for you to be an advocate for this test with your doctor if you want to get a better picture of which diseases and conditions you might develop.

Another exciting area of medicine involves understanding how we can actually modify our DNA at the molecular level. **Editas Medicine** is creating technology called "gene editing" that can turn on or off specific genes. It's still early in development and out of scope of the book, but it's a company worth following (editasmedicine.com).

Insider Tips

19. **Get your DNA mapped.** It is relatively cheap to get genotyped and easy to perform—it takes just swabbing the inside of your cheek.

20. **Consider finding a genetic counselor or online company to help you sort out which DNA test is the best.** It can be confusing to figure out which genomic company to go with.

New DNA Experts Will Guide You Through The Process

Over time scientists will figure out more correlations between genes, proteins, DNA, diseases, and outcomes. This will increase the complexity around gene testing. Given the complexity, I think new companies will emerge to help translate these findings for doctors and patients.

Generally, companies will offer two types of services: *genotyping*, which gives you a list of genes and variants, and *sequencing*, which takes your entire DNA and reads every component in detail (~3 billion of them). In computer language, sequencing is like identifying bits of data; genotyping is how an aggregate of these bits makes a computer perform a certain function.

Genotyping is usually less expensive than *sequencing*, which is significantly more time consuming. Genotyping also provides **your risk of disease**, whereas sequencing is more helpful to identify **specific unknown conditions**. For most purposes, you only need to know your genotype and this is what most consumer focused companies offer.

There are companies already working to make it easier for patients and doctors to connect with genomic health services. The following are some companies offering specialized genetic testing:

- **23andme** is probably the most well-known company in the group and has pioneered a direct-to-consumer service. With this information, patients can connect with genetic counselors and physicians to interpret the data. For about $99, you can have your DNA partially genotyped. The company provides a genotype profile that focuses on genealogy (for instance, if you are of Caucasian descent, you have an XX percent chance of getting diabetes). They offer a kit that you get in your home that provides the following at 23andme.com:

  — Reports on 240+ health conditions and traits
  — Testing for 40+ inherited conditions
  — Discovering your ancestry composition
  — Updating your DNA as science advances

- **Navigenics** (now with Life Technologies) utilizes a similar platform, but focuses more on preventive aspects and the risks of developing a disease. For example, a patient could discover that their genotype is associated with a higher risk for melanoma. The patient can present that information to their physician, who would then closely monitor any changes to their skin (lifetechnologies.com).

- **Pathway Genomics** differentiates itself by focusing on wellness, fitness, and how your genes play into these aspects of your life (pathway.com).

- **MolecularHealth** uses algorithms to analyze genomic data, clinical history, and published scientific evidence, with the goal of helping you make better therapy decisions (molecularhealth.com).

- **DNA Direct** offers more than 2,000 molecular diagnostic and genetic tests (dnadirect.com).

- **Biomeme** is a company that has built a device that allows your phone to become a mobile DNA lab (biomeme.com).

- **GeneDx** specializes in helping patients find out if they have inherited a rare disease. If a family member has a rare disease, now you can find out if you carry the gene for that disease. They have an extensive list of rare diseases that you can get tested for (genedx.com).

- **Invitae** is helping to lower the cost of getting your DNA sequenced; and in doing so you can find out if you have any genes that carry any significant hereditary disorder (invitae.com).

Over the next decade, we will learn a lot more, so be sure to check company websites for the latest offerings and learnings.

Researchers are actively investigating the genomic and genetic mechanisms behind a number of important medical conditions. I have compiled a list below of actively researched diseases that will eventually have genomic correlations so we can create interventions. I would encourage you to do your own research to stay up-to-date on:

- Osteoporosis
- Cystic fibrosis
- Stroke
- Blood clots
- Rheumatoid arthritis
- Psoriasis
- Lupus
- Schizophrenia
- Asthma
- Infertility
- Diabetes
- Obesity

In the near future, we all will need to know our genetic map at the DNA level. It will be part of our medical records. Doctors will ask for genetic histories (or offer these tests to patients) so they can make specific clinical recommendations. Google mapping your DNA, as the title suggests (and being a bit cheeky as well), is something we all should consider. It will become a cornerstone of prevention.

In the next chapter, we cover another important aspect of digital prevention—making sure we can heal ourselves. We now have the ability to actually fix ourselves by banking our healthy cells for later use. Using your own cells to fix problems takes customization to the extreme. Imagine using your *own* cells to repair your body.

11

IN THE END, YOU CAN FIX YOURSELF

That's right—you read the chapter title correctly. With new procedures and advances in stem cell research, clinicians can help you make specific repairs and heal yourself with the help of your own cells.

Stem cells, in short, are cells from your body that can transform into any other cell and **help repair worn-out tissues.** They are cells that have not yet decided what they will be when they grow up; they are undifferentiated. A stem cell can become a brain cell, heart cell, or liver cell. The stem cell makes this decision based on the chemicals that surround the cell, which promote organ development in one direction or another. However, as we get older, most of our cells have moved past the stem cell stage into adult cell stage; e.g., they have graduated to a liver cell.

regenerate organs and tissues. An extensive review of biobanking is beyond the scope of this book, but you can also learn more about banking adult stem cells at **CellTex**, which is a company hoping to bring stem cell therapy to the US market. Of note, banking is not usually covered by insurance, so costs can be high, but the benefits can be profound (celltexbank.com).

Insider Tips

21. **Plan to "bank" your cells**—as you age it can be a great resource to rebuild tissue.

22. **Using printed tissue, for worn-out parts,** will become one of the main ways for us to stay young. The process is still pretty pricey—but like with most things—the cost will come down.

Printing New Organs

Similar to what is happening with 3-D printing technology in general, we have the **technology to build organs cell by cell.** Scientists have also improved the ability to take a cell and grow more cells (called culturing). At present, machines are being developed that can take cells and create an organ layer by layer, using this technique. Harnessing 3-D printing techniques, the machine uses a nozzle to "print" out sheets of cells and hydrogel droplets that form a scaffold and mimic human tissue e.g., connective, muscle, and nerve tissues. Imagine if you could simply "print" out a new kidney for someone or create new skin for a burn victim. The possibilities stemming from this technology are endless:

- For children who need prosthetic limbs, they can get custom-fit devices each year at a fraction of the cost of traditional prosthetics.

- Prior to complex or high-risk procedures, surgeons can build a 3-D model of organs such as the brain or heart so they can fine-tune the procedure to the patient's organ.

Print New Organs—Cell By Cell

The advent of 3-D printing in manufacturing has had important consequences for medicine. You've probably heard of 3-D printers being used to make plastic objects, but have you considered their use for building body parts and organs? This technology began about a decade ago and has been used to build nerve, cardiac, and lung tissues. The hope is for 3-D printing to be used to build entire organs for patients in need of organ transplants.

This is how it's done: First, cells are obtained by biopsy or by using stem cells and then grown in a lab. After the cells have grown and multiplied, they are collected to form a special "ink" called **BioInk**. Specialized printers are loaded with BioInk and another compound called hydrogel, a placeholder that forms a sort of scaffold for the BioInk to be printed on. As layers of BioInk are laid down one on top of the other, they fuse together. The hydrogel "scaffold" ensures that everything is kept in its intended place so a specific shape, such as the hollow tube of a blood vessel, can be formed. Tissue is then left in a special growth medium for several weeks, allowing it to mature and for the hydrogel to dissolve. After maturation, the tissue is ready for use.

Bank Your Kid's Cells For Later Use

The industry around the banking of stem cells is growing quickly. The basic concept is that **by saving good cells now**, when you need new cells (or organs or tissue), you can have a reservoir to take from. Given the ease of finding cell banks online or just asking your doctor, the era of consumers (like you) driving biobanking is here.

A great source of stems cells is found when we are born—inside the umbilical cord. Stem cells in cord blood can be banked privately or publicly; both options are regulated by the Food and Drug Administration. Currently, the National Cord Blood Program is the largest non-profit public cord-blood donation program. And the largest private program is the Cord Blood Registry.

If you are planning to have a baby, it could be very important to open a stem cell bank account on your child's behalf. Stem cells are easily retrieved from the umbilical cord at birth and can be saved. In the future, if your child unfortunately needs a new organ, doctors can use these stem cells to create one. Most hospitals now offer cord-blood banking services.

As the chapter title suggests, we will need to start preparing for aging in a whole new way—**one in which we will need to expect that we may need replacement parts**. The science and technology are already available for some organs (liver, heart, cartilage) and no doubt will continue to expand. Given the potential for improving the quality of life as you age, it is important to learn about this category of medicine. I would encourage you to stay tuned as more research comes out and more companies and hospitals enter the field to provide these services.

12

MAKE PUBLIC HEALTH YOUR DIGITAL ALLY

C ontagion, the Matt Damon movie, highlights the critical importance of having a public health system that is proactive and pre-emptive. The movie has a typical doomsday scenario of an airborne virus that is about to kill millions. It, however, is not a far-fetched scenario dreamed up by Hollywood filmmakers. In fact, something similar happened in 1918 with the Spanish flu; 500 million got sick and nearly 50 million died. More recently, news of the Ebola virus has caused a similar interest in making our public health programs more vigilant and ready.

Most of us do not worry about epidemics, however. We worry about the safety of food at restaurants, the pollution in the air triggering our asthma, and the amount of toxic metals in the water supply. How do we build a better public health system—one that delivers services faster, better, smarter, and cheaper? How do we move the system from being often reactive to pre-emptive? How do we move our focus from broad prevention strategies to one that involves more targeted surveillance and intervention? I think digital technologies can also make public health more effective and efficient. In fact, public health officials have taken the lead by investing millions in technologies to improve service operations.

In the ER, we see this often with outbreaks. One patient gets sick with a bad case of the flu. And then 2, 3, 4. Before too long, patients with the flu are coming in droves. In the early stages, cases show up at different hospitals. If we could capture outbreak information across hospitals, we could more quickly identify the source of the problem and take necessary steps to ensure the "outbreak" is contained.

Insider Tips

23. **Know your local public health resources.** You will be surprised at the breadth and depth of public health programs. In whatever community you live in, research the local and state public health department websites for information on new technologies that are being used to improve health services. Often they will have information on pregnancy, asthma, diabetes, HIV, and other conditions. This information can be helpful to your extended family or neighbors, even if you do not have a specific condition.

24. **Become aware of public health surveillance technologies.** New diagnostics will enable us to monitor infectious diseases earlier and prevent outbreaks. In the future your boss might have you take a flu test at home and, if positive, not come in to work.

Startups are also getting into the public health game. **Fount.in** has developed a program to analyze Twitter feeds to determine which parts of a city may be sicker than others in real time. It's like a local disease radar that's similar to the Storm Tracker you see on the Weather Channel. Use Fount.in to find out which parts of a city are germ hotspots so you can avoid those areas or avoid handshakes for the day (humanaut.is/projects/germtracker). Another organization, **HealthMap**, provides data on local outbreaks of disease (healthmap.org).

Healthvana is improving the way you can interact with public health and sexual health clinics by making a simple thing like getting test results much quicker and more reliable. They can also help you find a place to get tested for HIV and STDs in a Yelp like manner (healthvana.com).

One of the emerging ways to create surveillance is to set up shop in places where sick people congregate. In the next section, we will discuss ways in which health institutions can help create better infectious disease surveillance strategies so you won't get sick when you go to the hospital. It is important to know what your local hospital is doing about this issue.

Getting "Checked Out" Before Checking In

Although not widely publicized, it is easy for patients to carry harmful organisms into a hospital that can spread to other patients. **MRSA (methicillin-resistant Staphylococcus aureus)** is one of those organisms, which has caught public attention because it has caused some people to have amputations and contributed to numerous deaths.

The issue is that we may carry the MRSA bacteria, but aren't aware of it. Some scientists estimate that 1 out of 4 people carry MRSA in their nasal passages. So why don't we get more people tested before they walk into the hospital? What if you go into a hospital and in the bed next to you is a patient carrying MRSA who has not been diagnosed yet? Or even more concerning, what if you are that patient carrying MRSA and don't know it?

The approach to managing patients carrying diseases into the hospital is changing. New digital technologies will quickly identify pathogens, **allowing for patients to be screened "at the door."** For example, Becton Dickinson and other companies have already developed instruments that take blood samples or a swab from the skin to determine the presence of MRSA within two hours (bd.com/geneohm).

Some hospitals are already on board with MRSA testing and test all patients entering high-risk areas like the ICU to prevent MRSA outbreaks. These proactive surveillance programs are being used to screen patients in ICUs and those undergoing high-risk surgeries, such as cardiac bypass, to dramatically reduce the number of MRSA infections. At Evanston Hospital in Illinois, patients are tested before they are admitted. Those who test positive are quarantined to dedicated areas of the hospital to reduce the spread of disease.

Another company, **nanoRETE**, developed a method to rapidly detect pathogens using a handheld device that can generate screening results in a few hours at a significantly lower cost than traditional methods. Initial applications of the technology are targeted toward mobile diagnosis of tuberculosis and detection of harmful bacteria in food (nanorete.com).

Will The TSA Check You For Viruses Too?

Other areas for surveillance are places where we all converge and interact with people from around the globe. One of the easiest and fastest ways for diseases to get from one place to another is by routine travel. Consider that about 8 million people travel by air each day and can carry diseases across borders.[11]

You may have heard that some diseases start in animals and mutate, spreading to humans. They can be serious and even fatal (consider swine flu, bird flu, and SARS.) Our bodies are not well equipped to combat these novel illnesses.

Across the globe, health systems have been tapping into airport processes to try to screen people for diseases. Airports in many Asian countries have installed heat monitors to screen passengers who may have a fever before boarding the plane.

The international airport in Hong Kong employs fever monitors and requires arriving passengers to walk through body-heat scanners that resemble metal detectors to measure body temperature. If a body temperature registers at 100 degrees or more, the passenger goes through a secondary screening, such as a throat examination, and may be detained and taken to a clinic for observation. Airports in Indonesia, Malaysia, and Taiwan are also using similar technology in an attempt to curtail the spread of communicable diseases.

Analyte Health:
Building a Better Preventive Health System

Analtye Health is on a mission to help people get tested for HIV, hepatitis, STDs, and other wellness tests. Now the nation's largest online diagnostic testing company, Analyte has built an online version of what public health clinics offer. Analyte's platform goes one step further. Instead of standing in line at a clinic, consumers get the benefit of privacy and anonymity of testing online. The results have been dramatic.

The rates of disease identification are 2 to 3 times **higher** than the standard primary care clinic, while the costs are 2 to 3 times **lower** than a typical clinic.

By making it easy and accessible, more people are getting tested earlier in the course of the disease process and thus are less likely to spread the disease—a win for the public at large.

Digital Prevention Summary

In this section, I laid out a framework to help you **embrace the tools and technologies that will prevent illness** or catch it early enough so it does not impact your life significantly. We must learn to change **our "wait till something breaks"** mindset to one that is **proactive and involves personal leadership.** You can easily become an educated partner with the right websites and apps. You can take advantage of new diagnostics and sensors now being created to stay ahead of the disease process. There is a real opportunity for you to transform your prevention game plan with digital innovations.

Unfortunately, in the ER, I see the opposite every day. It's the 50-year-old man who has had chest pain for a few days but ignores this warning sign and waits to be rushed in on a gurney because he's in cardiac arrest! In fact, by the time he experienced the initial symptoms, he was well into the disease process. It's the 20-year-old female who has poorly controlled diabetes and starts antibiotics too late for a simple kidney infection. The infection triggers her diabetes to go into diabetic ketoacidosis, a serious life-threatening condition, causing her to end up in the intensive care unit.

Our bodies are complicated machines. We need to actively monitor the health of our bodies, organs, and cells. And today the science of cellular surveillance is a reality. The good news is that we have the technology, science, and, most importantly, a consumer opportunity to make this a reality.

You must engage with these new technologies. They *will spare you* from suffering unnecessary expenses and possibly premature death. Collectively, more proactive patients will drive down the disease burden in the US. I believe this is one **significant way you can save our healthcare system**. Below are some important highlights to consider.

Digital Prevention Highlights:

1. We need a **consumer revolution** in healthcare that empowers patients.
2. The biggest revolution in medicine **will happen inside** our cells. Our blood and other cells provide the pathway for monitoring and predicting disease.
3. As patients, we all need to **shift our mindset**. It's important to get your friends and family to become aware of the need to become active co-pilots in managing our care.
4. Doctors currently don't typically tailor recommendations to what is happening inside your cells and blood. Risk factors like high blood pressure, family history, high cholesterol, smoking, and diabetes can only go so **far in pinpointing those most at risk**.
5. We can add alarms to our bodies. Low-cost sensors and manufacturing technologies have led to the integration of medical devices into many commonly used products.
6. We can **speak up and ask for more** from our healthcare system. We must ask our doctors, hospital administrators, and medical researchers to individualize care even more.
7. We now have the **ability to actually fix ourselves** by banking our healthy cells for later use—this is the ultimate extension of precision medicine.
8. Public health has traditionally been focused on broad prevention versus more targeted surveillance and intervention. New tools will empower public health organizations, pre-empting disease for all of us.

SECTION III:

DIGITAL OPTIMIZATION

13

THE NEED FOR SPEED

Healthcare is now all around us—it happens on our smartphones, at the grocery store, at the workplace, and even in some airports. The growing number of access points will lead to faster care and, in many cases, will improve outcomes as people start therapy sooner—if you **learn how and when to use these new access points**.

Moreover, new technologies and digital innovations are allowing clinics to be squeezed into smaller footprints—e.g., the instruments used to analyze blood are shrinking to the size of handheld machines. This will ultimately result in allowing us to **carry a virtual clinic in our pockets**.

The reason this is important is that too many of us sit on the sidelines thinking accessing care is too cumbersome and painful to get through. It can take weeks just to see a doctor or get a second opinion for a diagnosis. Seeing a doctor will most often result in the need to then go to a lab and then return to the doctor's office just to discuss your results.

Since you have more options to access care, the next question is **where should you start?** This chapter will give you a framework to consider when accessing the new delivery points and to help accelerate your healthcare. We will cover:

- The new meaning of house calls
- Mental health deep dive
- Retail-based care
- Workplace-based care

Many of us have already begun to engage with this new delivery platform, from pharmacy and employer clinics, to telemedical visits and other remote health services. According to the PEW research group, about 35% of US adults use the Internet to streamline online diagnoses.[12] This new approach centers care around you, and integrates into your life in an efficient way. Insurers are taking notice and encouraging visits to these clinics and telemedical organizations. We are in the beginning stages of an important transformation. Smart Patients will need to **understand how to best engage with various delivery models.**

Insider Tips

25. **More health systems and insurers are offering telehealth options**—so check what your provider offers. Telehealth companies are quickly changing and offering new conveniences.

26. **Think of having a "portfolio" of digital access options—** perhaps 10% telehealth, 10% pharmacy clinics, 20% employer clinics, and 60% traditional care.

The New Meaning Of House Calls

In the beginning, doctors primarily made house calls because it was difficult for sick patients to travel to them. This changed to our current system where the sick travel to doctors.

Now telemedical companies allow a doctor to be in one city and the patient in another. These virtual visits are facilitated by add-on devices such as a **digital stethoscope** that can record heart and lung sounds. High-definition video cameras also provide the ability to evaluate the skin for rashes or lesions. **Virtual gloves** allow doctors to examine the abdomen. Today a nearly complete physical exam can be done remotely; physicians and patients can both stay at home but still see each other!

Virtual care is also being **integrated into the pathway of the traditional care model.** For example, after being released from the hospital following surgery, you can snap a picture of the surgical incision, send it via your phone, and have a follow-up visit all in the convenience of your home without even leaving your bed.

Telemedicine encompasses a number of alternative ways to get healthcare:

1. **Connect with centers of excellence;** e.g., Mayo, Hopkins, Cleveland, Harvard, Stanford Hospital, etc.
2. **Get second opinion consults**
3. **Get diagnosed online**
4. **See a doctor online**

It is important to remember that you will have options in the digital age through these platforms that did not exist in the past. So if you happen to be faced with a health issue, take advantage of the ways that hospitals and providers are now interacting with patients.

Connect With "Centers Of Excellence"

Many of you do not live near a major medical center or are in an area with very few specialists. Most major health systems offer telemedical services to attract patients who live in rural and ex-urban areas. Below are a few nationally recognized leaders in healthcare and some ways they are engaging patients through the web:

- **Mayo Clinic's** comprehensive website can give you more information on a variety of medical concerns: diseases, symptoms, drugs, lab tests, procedures, and even general health information. All of the information is compiled and written to be easily understood (mayoclinic.com).

- **Cleveland Clinic** offers a variety of self-serve medical information. Take quizzes, read articles on health and wellness, and sign up for newsletters. You can also interact with the clinic digitally; e.g., review of your CT scan, getting an e-consult, or reviewing your chart—all through their website (my.clevelandclinic.org).

- **Johns Hopkins** offers health information and the ability to inter-act with their institution online. Research physicians, schedule appointments, and read reviews (hopkinsmedicine.org).

- **Massachusetts General Hospital** offers a great portal of general health education and an easy way to search for medical research going on at the institution. This is very helpful if you have a specific medical condition and you want to get more details about how you can get involved with clinical research and finding a doctor (massgeneral.org).

- **Stanford Medicine's** website allows you to get an overview of their centers of excellence, such as the Cancer Institute, Heart Center, Neurosciences, Orthopedics, Surgical Services, and Transplantation. Stanford Healthcare provides an easy search tool to help you find the information you are looking for (stanfordmedicine.org & stanfordhealthcare. org).

- **Beth Israel Deaconess Medical Center's** page is set up like a blog-type medical portal. Read up on their highly specialized health centers like the Digestive Disease Center. They utilize quizzes, videos, and a lot of links to other sites of interest to make the whole process easy to use and interesting (bidmc.org).

Get A Second Opinion

Patients may also be interested in getting a second opinion for certain conditions that require specialty assessment. A number of new companies specialize in transmission of health information, enabling you to send all of your medical records electronically and privately to another physician.

- **iRapidConsult** focuses on back and spine treatment options from neurosurgeons and spine surgeons. Upload an MRI of your back and then receive an online consult with a spine surgeon and get a medical report within a week (iRapidConsult.com).

- **Grand Rounds** provides a specialist and a report based on the latest scientific research (grandroundshealth.com).

- **MetaMed** conducts medical research for the patient. A team of research professionals finds all the information relevant to you, considering your full medical history, your genetics, and other personal health information (metamed. com).

- **Advance Medical** is one of the oldest providers and has been in business since 1999 (advance-medical.com).

- **2nd.MD** offers consultation from 2 to 5 specialists, in a 20-minute phone or video-conference session. Patients then get a written summary of the conversation (2nd.md).

Get Diagnosed Online

A number of companies enable you to get diagnostic tests and services (like blood work, urinalysis, or an MRI) through a web-based platform without ever physically seeing a doctor.

- **Analyte Health** allows patients to access preventive diagnostics such as hepatitis C screening through an online portal. Patients can get diagnosed without the hassle of having to go to a doctor's office first. Analyte will also connect you to a specialist if you need one (analytehealth. com).

- At **Direct Dermatology** you can describe your symptoms and upload a photo of a rash, lesion, or area of concern for a dermatologist to review. The company eliminates lengthy wait times for an appointment (directdermatology.com).

- **Spruce Health** allows you to describe your acne, take a picture, and get a response within 24 hours by a board-certified dermatologist who will review your case and create your personal treatment plan with appropriate prescriptions (sprucehealth.com).

- **DermLink** uses your phone, iPad, or digital camera to help diagnose skin conditions. You take a picture and get a diagnosis and even treatment from a doctor within 24 hours (dermlink.md).

- **Zipnosis** allows you to get diagnosed and treated for minor health problems by simply filling out a form (zipnosis.com).

See A Doctor Online

You now have the option to see a primary care physician or even a specialist online without ever setting foot in their office. Many insurance companies are starting to embrace this trend. Many health plans now include this benefit to cover a number of minor conditions like colds, flus, urinary tract infections, sinusitis, etc.

To see a doctor online, check out these companies:

- **American Well** specializes in helping connect consumers to specialists and has developed an online platform for doctor's visits. Patients create an account, input their health history, answer a short questionnaire, choose a physician from a list of providers, and then are connected to the physician of their choice through live video chat (americanwell.com).

- **Teladoc** is one of the largest telehealth providers for patients with non-emergency issues such as minor illnesses and can provide care while a patient is traveling internationally (teladoc.com).

- **Doctor on Demand** offers a quick and convenient way to speak to a doctor right from your phone for most primary care issues (doctorondemand.com).

- **MDLive** is another company that allows you to see a doctor online for common medical conditions (mdlive.com).

- **MDAligne** provides patients with access to physicians and nurses through an online chat and video consults or by telephone in most states. Different from other companies on this list, MDAligne also allows physicians to order necessary lab tests or diagnostic images. Patients pay discounted rates through MDAligne (mdaligne.com).

There are a number of other providers to check out as well, including **First Stop Health** (fshealth.com) and **iSelectMD** (iselectmd.com). I would recommend searching the Internet or checking my blog (**healthdisrupted.com**) to find the latest companies providing faster access.

Mental Health Enters The Age Of Telehealth

Mental health is one of the largest medical categories to benefit from telehealth. Telepsychology—seeing your mental health provider via your computer or mobile device—is providing better, immediate care to more patients. Because of the potential impact of telemedicine for mental health, we will take a deep dive into this specialty.

Mental disorders, including depression, are extraordinarily common in the US; about 19 million adults experience major depression every year[13] and 40 million have an anxiety disorder.[14] These disorders cost the business world about $80-100 billion annually in employee absenteeism.[15] And yet, only 1/3 of patients with anxiety and 1/2 of patients with depression get treatment.[16]

Telepsychology may be even better than traditional, in person care. For example, if you Skype with a therapist from the safety and comfort of your home, it's much easier to be open and honest as well as make and keep appointments since there is no traveling needed. Virtual models also allow for increased frequency of interactions, which can help patients when they are experiencing a "crisis" event. A study done by the Veterans Administration showed a 24% reduction in psychiatric admissions when telepsychology tools were used.[17]

This is important because there is a national shortage of nearly 30,000-40,000 psychiatrists and psychologists in the US.[18] Below are a few companies transforming how people are addressing mental health concerns and staying happy:

- **Breakthrough** (now with MDLive) allows you to find a therapist who can assist with your specific mental health issue and offers therapy sessions via video chat at home (breakthrough.com).

- **AbilTo** delivers behavioral coaching to patients who've experienced life-changing medical events. Their 8-week session is conducted via video chat and helps patients deal with life events like the loss of a loved one or getting back to work after giving birth (abilto.com).

- **Ginger.io** collects health activity information in the background, like your movement this week compared to last and the number of people you talked to. For patients with depression, this information can be a sign of how a patient is doing (ginger.io).

- **The Shedler QPD Panel** is a patient-administered automated mental health test that screens for depression and eight other psychiatric disorders (digitaldiagnostics. com).

- **Cantab Mobile** is a computerized testing program that can be administered by a nurse or other mid-level provider to diagnose cognitive disorders and dementia (cambridgecognition.com).

- **Neurotrack** has a computerized test that predicts the development of mild cognitive impairment and Alzheimer's disease years before symptoms appear (neurotrack.com).

- **Depressioncheck** has validated screening tools to assess your risk of depression, bipolar, and anxiety disorders in three minutes. After completing a short survey, you receive a confidential report sharing how many of these symptoms may be affecting you— check itunes.

Skype A Psychotherapist

Anna, a 32-year-old, has been struggling with depression for the past two years. She first noticed she was losing interest in things she normally loved doing. Anna started seeing a psychotherapist and began a treatment plan. She did not want to go on an antidepressant because she wanted to get pregnant and she had concerns about the side effects. However, she was having trouble fitting therapy sessions into her busy schedule. After missing two consecutive appointments, her symptoms began to return. Concerned about Anna's inability to adhere to her treatment plan, her psychotherapist suggested a trial of therapy sessions via Skype.

Anna's treatment has been more successful than ever. She no longer stresses about scheduling her sessions. Instead, she can now do sessions in her home, on her lunch break, or from a hotel room while traveling for work. Anna was able to avoid medications and felt better about getting pregnant.

Some people prefer to see an in person provider versus a virtual provider. For those individuals, there are a host of new, more convenient options. In the next section, we cover some of these options and discover how they are integrating into our daily lives.

Retail Stores Become Diagnostic & Triage Hubs

Healthcare is going retail and giving new meaning to "retail therapy" (no pun intended). Imagine seeing a medical provider or getting a diagnostic test in between shopping for groceries. Started only about 10 years ago, **retail clinics** in pharmacies and grocery stores will soon become a significant part of wellness and care for many.

This "retailization" of healthcare helps make care more convenient both in location (nearby, where you shop for groceries) and timing (some are open 24 hours). The value is clear. It doesn't require a special trip to the doctor's office. Wait times to see a retail provider are typically much lower. They provide health services such as flu shots, TB tests, school physicals, and evaluation of minor conditions such as fever, cough, sore throat, and urinary tract infections.

Pharmacies and grocery stores are excellent hubs for "retail care." Now you can find a **Take Care Clinic** (Walgreens) or a **Minute**

Clinic (CVS) in nearly a thousand stores. **Walgreens** is breaking new ground through a partnership with **Theranos**. Through this partnership, Walgreens will be able to process blood tests inside the store. Theranos' lab-in-a-box service is revolutionary because their machine can do nearly all the testing that you might get in a hospital, but it only requires a few drops of blood. Prices are also much lower—most tests are just a few dollars.

Walmart is advancing its healthcare relationship with its customers by increasing health services. Some Walmarts have low-priced clinics and lab-draw stations where you can get blood tests done while you shop. Recently, Walmart began installing health kiosks made by **SoloHealth**. Customers can visit the kiosk and check their blood pressure and weight, receive a vision screen, and get an overall health assessment. SoloHealth allows people to respond to questions from a health kiosk screener, input symptoms into a symptom checker, receive a report of their results, and gain access to a database of local doctors.

RiteAid is working with a company called **Higi** to provide in-store wellness assessments that include weight and blood pressure, so every time you visit the store you can check your vital signs and track them over time.

Get Well At Work

Employers are eagerly jumping into optimizing healthcare delivery. Employer clinics provide doctors, nurses, and other providers to employees inside the corporate setting. These clinics also manage wellness programs, providing a physical location for employees to get their blood sugar and blood pressure checked. With clinics in the workplace, employees are able to receive services in a convenient setting, which is likely to result in fewer sick days and greater productivity.

Employer clinics have been around since the '50s, but we are only now seeing widespread adoption of this concept. In fact, workplace clinics are quickly spreading across the US. According to Mercer Management, as of 2010, **15% of employers with 500+ employees had clinics in the workplace**, and another 10% are considering doing so in the next two years. United Airlines has recently announced opening a large employer clinic at O'Hare Airport to better serve its international and mobile workforce.

Clinics also provide a **financial intervention** for the company's performance. Employers know that health affects both the bottom line (the direct cost of care) and top line (because of lost productivity). Workers who show up to work but are sick and underproductive, a problem termed *presenteeism*, are estimated to cost companies as much as $40 to $100 billion each year.[19]

Companies also know that keeping their employees healthy is of strategic importance. Paradoxically, Starbucks spends more on health insurance than on coffee beans.[20] Likewise, one of the biggest costs for GM isn't anything to do with the production of cars; it's actually the cost of paying for health insurance for its workers. The CEO of GM mentioned in an article that the cost of insurance adds about $1,500 to the price of every car.[21]

Smart Patients need to become "Smart Employees." They need to understand their corporate wellness offerings and why it is important to engage in group wellness activities. Group based health interventions are showing real promise in improving adherence to wellness goals and helping people achieve their individual health goals. This is explored in more detail in the section on social health.

Employers are getting more courageous and creative. Previously, they shied away from "intervening" in an employee's health habits. Researchers have changed this sentiment. Safeway ties its employees' healthcare premiums, up to 30%, to how well employees participate in wellness programs. Safeway has successfully built financial incentives to curb costs and is one of the few employers that have not seen a significant increase in healthcare expenditures over the past 5 years.[22]

There is growing evidence suggesting that interventions should be developed at the local level, customizing programs to geography, culture, gender, and even employee type. So employees in Wyoming might get different services than ones in Florida.

Employers are also focusing on healthier behavior changes. A number of employers have placed treadmill desks with built-in laptops so that their employees can exercise and work at the same time. They are also paying employees to pick healthier foods, attend nutrition seminars, and adhere to workplace health standards.

Premise Health is the largest employer clinic operator in the country with over 500 work sites and aims to transform employee health by delivering clinical innovations where you work (premisehealth.com).

Wellness has become the hottest area for digital health. For example, **Limeade** has created an engagement platform that builds on existing employer and plan services, integrating biometric screenings, onsite services and seminars, health coaching, and targeted programs for specific conditions and behaviors. They also tie into broader culture-building and talent initiatives. Employees can set goals and monitor their progress; employers can review their progress and performance (limeade.com).

Keas.com is another leader in workplace wellness. Keas focuses on meaningful goals for employees, which in turn will keep employees motivated in wellness programs (keas.com).

The Doctor Will See You At Work

Mary, a 27-year-old Google employee, was wrapped up in her work; the last thing she was concerned about was a sore throat. But when the sore throat persisted and she started to feel feverish, she decided to stop by the clinic in her office building. Google is part of a growing number of companies with doctors and clinics on-site. The physician was concerned that she may have strep throat. A throat swab confirmed that it was strep.

Mary received the antibiotics she needed from the Google clinic. But the doctor noticed she also had some swelling around her tonsils. The strep throat had grown into an abscess, so the doctor arranged for her to see an ENT specialist virtually with the aid of an intra-oral camera that the clinic had. The specialist was able to see Mary's entire mouth and confirmed that it was an abscess. Mary needed to have the abscess drained in addition to the antibiotics she had received. This quick visit to the workplace clinic prevented what could have developed into a much more complicated health situation for her.

To optimize care in the digital age, we need to transform how we access healthcare from one that is **doctor-centric** to one that is **patient-centric**. It requires collaboration from doctors, hospitals, employers, retail centers, insurers, and patients. It is critical for you to champion a move toward faster, more streamlined healthcare.

Ultimately, when care moves into a distributed format, it improves both speed and access, but it also requires a mind shift from patients to rethink when and how they access care. Over the next decade, the need for speed will be increasingly critical. Given provider shortages, we will likely see a systemic slowdown. So in this era as a Smart Patient you will need to learn this new engagement paradigm.

14

THE PRICE IS RIGHT
(OR AT LEAST TRANSPARENT)

L earning to shop for healthcare will be the most critical new skill for all of us to learn. Most people don't shop—they don't ask their doctors to find the lowest-cost place to get a prescription filled. They don't have an easy way to pick the lowest-cost imaging center for a CT scan. They usually don't ask how much a hospital admission will cost even for something planned like a pregnancy.

Shopping for healthcare is hard because it lacks transparency. It is difficult to make apples-to-apples comparison...like are gallbladder surgeries in one hospital the same as another?

But ultimately, shopping for health is more like buying a house versus buying diapers online. There are a lot of different factors to consider and it is important to get educated. Most people go through an extensive learning process to buy a house. What is the best mortgage type? What are important structural considerations? You should do the same level of diligence when obtaining medical care.

When shopping, it is **not only the price, but the overall costs** that you might incur across categories such as provider costs, lab tests, radiology, hospitalization, pharmaceutical costs, and surgical costs. For example, a doctor may give you a prescription for a CT scan of your abdomen. Most of us just go to the local hospital radiology department. But in truth, the cost of a CT scan can vary from $400 to $1,400 among various hospitals and outpatient imaging centers. So even if you have insurance, you may have a high deductible or co-insurance and end up paying a significant amount—another reason why it is important for you to become a good shopper.

With the Internet, you can shop for just about anything, from airplane tickets to groceries. When it comes to healthcare, however, there is no Kayak.com yet. As consumers start to share pricing information and **as programs develop to compare price, quality, and customer service,** we will start to see the power of the network and better price transparency.

Moreover, as quality standardizes over time, we will start to see more "commoditization"—meaning that in general you are going to have nearly the same experience and outcome for common health events like tonsillectomies, appendicitis surgery, annual physicals, acne treatment, etc. And as this occurs, it will then become easier to compare the cost and customer service for different health procedures. In this new era, you will not want to overspend. And to reiterate, the importance of learning how to become a better healthcare shopper will be critical.

Recently a non-profit, **The Health Care Cost Institute,** has launched **Guroo.com**—a website listing cost information for more than 70 common health conditions and services. The data, however, is relatively unique because it comes directly from major insurers, making the accuracy of cost much better.

Also some new companies providing price information are Healthcare Blue Book and Health In Reach as discussed below.

Insider Tips

27. **Check prices before you get care—this process will soon become easier.** Insurers and the government will make sure price transparency becomes one of the hottest areas in healthcare.

28. **Negotiate when you can.** Many providers are becoming savvier to working with patients, especially if you can cite how much care costs at a nearby hospital. Price variation across health services, prescription drugs, and hospital stays fluctuates as **much as 30-50%**, so this area is ripe for change.

Many new companies are emerging. The following companies can help you get deals:

Prescription Deals

- **GoodRx** allows patients to find the best prices for drugs, which are particularly helpful if you don't have insurance, or have a high co-pay for medications. Find the best deal before you even leave the doctor's office so you know which pharmacy to go to (goodrx.com).

Free Care And Discount Drugs

- **Needymeds** is a non-profit that provides a list of free and discount clinics (needymeds.org).

Negotiate With Doctors & Hospitals

- **PokitDok** is a health marketplace where consumers can search by condition or specialty and request a price quote directly from providers (pokitdok.com).

Manage Co-Pays And Deductibles

- **Simplee.com** and **CakeHealth.com** help patients' link health plans and health spending accounts to easily track and pay medical bills.

Compare Prices

- **Healthcare Blue Book** provides cost comparisons for medical treatments and services (healthcarebluebook.com).

- **Health In Reach** focuses on dentists and doctor costs (healthinereach.com).

- **NerdWallet** offers a hospital cost comparison tool so you can find out what local hospitals charge for procedures like knee surgery (nerdwallet.com).

- **Compass Professional Health Services** provides concierge level advice on how to lower costs for employees of their corporate customers. For example, they will help you discover and compare the total cost of knee surgery but also identify in-network surgeons, anesthesiologists and hospitals (compassphs.com).

- **Castlight Health and HealthSparq** allow employees at their client companies to search prices for office visits to doctors, lab work, and other services. It provides corresponding out-of-pocket cost calculation and quality metrics (castlighthealth.com, healthsparq.com).

- **Guroo.com**, as mentioned, pulls data from Aetna, Assurant Health, Humana, and UnitedHealth, and is free and open to anyone.

- **ReferMe Health** offers prices and comparison shopping for procedures and hospitals (refermehealth.com).

The hope is that consumers will demand more cost transparency especially when they have to pay more of the bill. In the coming decade, as companies shift more of the cost to employees through higher co-pays and deductibles, this information will have to become more available and transparent.

What's Up With The Price?

Healthcare prices can vary based on a number of factors such as region of the country, academic versus community hospitals, and pricing approaches (e.g., list high and discount) by individual doctors and hospitals. Across the country you might see a **50% variation in what one provider will charge versus another for a similar procedure.**[23] Given the variation, it is likely that you might pay more for the same procedure than your counterpart at a different hospital or location.

For example, the cost difference to deliver a baby can vary between $9,000 and $17,000 for an uncomplicated delivery.[24] This nearly 100% price difference is financially important because you will likely pay some percentage of this cost through co-insurance, co-pays, and deductibles. **CostHelper.com** estimates that patients pay between $500 and $3,000 for a normal delivery. Many other hospital procedures have similar differences to consider.

Finding the best value will become ever more important, especially as **many Americans move towards using high-deductible health plans.** The best value provides the right outcome at the right time and at the right price—but this may not be the lowest-priced option. As you know, when it comes to your health, just looking for the lowest price won't always yield the best (or safest) results. Unfortunately, this means that **all of us will need to spend more time to become educated.** Thankfully new digital technologies and entrepreneurs will help make this process easier.

15

USE THE DOCTOR IN YOUR POCKET

We now live in an era where our phones and wearable devices will play a critical role in our health—especially for people with chronic conditions.

How we use our phones has changed dramatically. We can now unlock our car doors remotely via our phones. We can use our phones to monitor how long we brush our teeth, with **Beam Technologies'** Bluetooth-enabled toothbrush!

More computing power, smaller footprints, and increasing connectivity will allow more care to be managed or co-managed by the patient. In this chapter we'll focus on the **smartphone and other portable devices as a health platform** to deliver care and engage patients. Smartphones, in fact, are powerful, portable computers. They have inputs like a microphone and a camera that allow for two-way communication between providers and patients.

We will also discuss how smart devices are taking the "brain of a doctor" and translating it into various gadgets and applications that can be used by everyday people.

Finally, we will talk about how easily accessible devices will create opportunities for patients to get more quickly diagnosed, in many cases from the comfort of their homes. Integrating these platforms into your daily life is especially important for people with chronic diseases like diabetes or heart disease.

Insider Tips

29. **Devices can virtualize your health experience.** Especially if you have a chronic disease, it is important to learn how to integrate these devices into your health management process.

30. **Your phone and home will become a health hub.** Various stakeholders, from hospitals and the government to insurers and tech companies, will want to produce new health products that can be used in the home—primarily because it will help lower costs.

Smartphones Become The Personal Health Hub

Smartphones are becoming the *de facto* platform for health and wellness. By platform, I mean that it can be deployed in different ways—educating, monitoring, treating, and communicating. Acting as a hub, **smartphones will connect with a number of other devices, creating an extended health platform.**

These devices will also be a convenient way to instantly receive health information like drug interactions, cardiac events, or low blood sugar levels. These future innovations will serve as a human "check engine light," alerting you if something is wrong.

Moreover, we carry our mobile devices with us everywhere. This allows smartphones to be uniquely used to collect health data and connect patients with health providers in real time. You can record the number of times you have symptoms, such as headaches, depression, and anxiety. This stored data can be shared with your doctor at a later date. I think we have all experienced the frustration of forgetting elements of symptoms we wanted to share with our doctors. Having a convenient record of symptoms could help eliminate that.

To add some color, let's talk about Tim: He's a 36-year-old hedge fund manager who is also a marathon runner. He has a family history of heart disease. His father died at 50 from sudden cardiac arrest and he worries the same fate may befall him. He begins by wearing the "undershirt of the future," which has thin wires and electrodes that measure heart rhythm. The shirt communicates with his smartphone and can make a 911 emergency call if there is a problem (like if he is unconscious). Think of your phone connected to a wired Under Armour shirt. This technology can also analyze Tim's heart rhythm to provide alerts and can even shock him if it senses a dangerous rhythm.

The good news is that a number of companies are working on developing wearable technologies that can interact with your phone. Here are some cool and innovative companies building the future of the smartphone as a health platform:

Ear & Eye
- **Cellscope** offers a device that attaches to your smartphone to **diagnose ear infections right at home.** You snap it to

the camera of your phone, and with it you can look at the eardrum of your child and then send a picture to a physician to get a diagnosis and potentially receive antibiotics. This saves a lot of time, and you avoid the hassle of having to go to your pediatrician's office (cellscope.com).

- **EyeNetra** is a device that fits onto a phone's camera to measure key parameters of the eye so patients can get prescription glasses without having to go see an optometrist or ophthalmologist. This company is working on helping 2.4 billion people globally who need eyeglasses but are currently without (eyenetra.com).

Diabetes Management

- **AgaMatrix** has developed the first FDA-approved glucometer that fits on an iPhone. This device is small and easily integrates into the form and look of the iPhone. Diabetics using it won't have to carry a separate machine to monitor their glucose levels, and it stores up to 300 test results, allowing for easy monitoring of glucose levels over time (agamatrix.com).

- **Cellnovo, Glooko, HealthPal, Telcare, and Entra Health** all have programs that capture glucose information from glucose meters and communicate that information to your phone and then to the Internet, where your health team can review it. Their services allow you to manage diabetes without having to write down and transfer information— meaning no pens and paper (cellnovo.com, glooko.com, myhealthpal.com, telcare.com, entrahealthsystems.com).

- **Biorasis** has developed the capability for long-term, real time glucose and metabolic monitoring using its device

Glucowizard. This implantable biosensor is a miniature glucometer that reads glucose levels, but is also capable of monitoring oxygen, carbon dioxide, and other metabolites (bio-orasis.com).

For Babies

Some infants need more care than others because they may be born with certain conditions that need monitoring, such as an irregular heartbeat or frequent urinary tract infections. The companies below are innovating on baby care:

- Developed by **Pixie Scientific**, Smart Diapers are disposable diapers that can keep track of your baby's health by monitoring for urinary tract infections, prolonged dehydration, and chronic kidney conditions. Who knew dirty diapers could offer insight into your baby's health (pixiescientific.com)?

- Withings **Smart Baby Monitor** allows parents to monitor their infant with audio and visual input anywhere there is a wireless connection. Alerts can be set and adapted to what parents would like to monitor (sleep disruption, fidgeting, room temperature, humidity). Connection to your smartphone allows for two-way communication between baby and parents. Music from your phone can also be played through the monitor, and you can remotely set it to project a soothing light display (withings.com).

- **Rest Devices** has created the smart cloth onesie. The device is woven into the clothing so it does not look like a medical product. It can record respiration, sleep, and temperature, and parents can view the data on their smartphone (mimobaby.com).

- **Teddy The Guardian** is a teddy bear that collects important health information as your child interacts with it. Teddy has sensors that measure a child's pulse, blood pressure, body temperature, and oxygen saturation when the child touches the bear's paw (teddytheguardian.com).

Monitoring The Heart And Heart Rate

- **AliveCor** is a device that attaches to your phone that allows you to capture an EKG and send it to your doctor. It can also detect if you are experiencing atrial fibrillation, which is a common form of cardiac arrhythmia. It is helpful for people who have palpitations or are at risk for an irregular heartbeat. The associated app, AliveECG, allows you to store all of your recordings so they can be compared over time by your physician (alivecor.com).

- **Withings** has developed a Smart Body Analyzer that resembles a weight scale. Users stand on it and it measures weight, body composition, heart rate, and even indoor air quality. The data is sent to a user's smartphone and stored so these metrics can be monitored over time (withings.com).

- **iHealth** has developed a number of user-friendly medical devices: a body analysis scale, wireless glucometer, pulse oximeter, and blood pressure and heart rate monitor (ihealthlabs.com).

For Your Elder Parents

- **Lively** is a digital monitoring platform designed to assist elderly people to "age in place" (stay in their homes as long as possible). Lively comes with several trackers: one for the fridge, a patient's pillbox, keys, and one that is customizable (for the bathroom door, a favorite chair, or exercise equipment). Data on the number of times a patient takes a medication, opens the fridge, leaves the house, etc. is recorded and uploaded to an app. Family members remotely see which areas the elder parent is doing well in and which ones need improvement. I think this creates greater peace of mind for adults caring for aging parents (mylively.com).

Faster Blood Sugar Control Can Improve Your Life

Ryan, a 45-year-old lawyer, has been struggling with diabetes since he was first diagnosed six years ago. He has been unable to manage his weight, diet, or blood sugar levels. Several weeks ago he skipped breakfast, rushing out of the house to make it to work on time. Soon after, he started feeling light-headed, but he wrote it off as stress due to a case he was working on. He began to feel sweaty, so he opened the office window to get some fresh air. When his co-worker, Bill, stopped by after lunch, he was shocked to see how pale Ryan looked. He was showing signs of hypoglycemia. Ryan checked and his blood sugar level was 49. Ryan quickly ate lunch and started to feel better.

This scenario was entirely avoidable. Although he has had the disease for six years, Ryan still finds it hard to understand how his behavior affects his blood sugar levels. He does not fully grasp how skipping a meal in the morning or exercising in the afternoon affects his blood sugar. Ryan decided to have an implantable insulin pump put in. He can program it to provide the right amount of insulin based on his busy lifestyle.

On workout days, he changes the program on the pump. He no longer has low drops or high jumps in his blood sugar because the device gives him a sense of control over his chronic illness without disrupting his daily routine.

We are definitely in a **new device-driven era of medicine.** These innovations will give us the ability to take better care of ourselves. Many of these companies will change and evolve, and new ones will emerge, but I hope to have provided you with a snapshot of how the future of healthcare might look. Most importantly, these new devices will dramatically speed up and improve our care.

16

PLUG INTO PATIENT NETWORKS

S ocial networks have taken our culture by storm. With Facebook, Yelp, Google Plus, chatting, and text messaging, it's hard to feel isolated. Moreover, we have all seen how networking technologies can provide greater efficiency to our lives—Skyping friends, managing parties through Evites, and even using Facebook to get recommendations for a new car. This level of connectivity gives us better and more useful information.

Now, using this phenomenon of social networking, patients can more easily connect with each other and **get answers, review new options,** and potentially pave **a path to more efficient care.** Let's say you have a child with epilepsy. You may have a lot of questions, and each day you come up with new ones. With a website where other parents share information, such as tips about seizure warning signs and managing medications, you could find real world answers and have more informed conversations with your doctor. The information might even help you avoid a doctor's visit and the expensive co-pay to see a specialist.

This is the power of online patient networks—they are always accessible and can at times provide more precise content and tips than what you get from your physician. Also, if you or your child has a rare disease, finding others who are sharing the same medical journey is an important aspect of healing. In this digital age of medicine, it is easier than ever for patients with rare conditions to connect with each other.

Historically, our health system, however, does not make it easy for people to find information. When was the last time your doctor told you, "Here is a website to help you find lower-cost prescription drugs"? Doctors may not think of this because most of them have very limited training on how to think like a patient.

Patients are beginning to see the true **power they have to provide help to each other**. Tech groups call this *crowdsourcing*, or using the power of *"the network"* to reach a goal. Now is the time to use our connections to help us heal and stay healthy.

Insider Tips

31. **Many disease conditions, both common and rare, have patient networks.** It's a matter of digging on the Internet for the one that suits you best.

32. **Using patient networks can lower costs** because you can quickly learn what works from other patients who have been through the process already. **Find networking sites that monitor** communication using clinically trained providers to ensure that you are getting the highest-quality information.

Sharing Is Caring

Patients interacting and helping each other will become a cornerstone of health delivery and provide "social healing."

Science shows how social connections improve our health. Patients who have chronic diseases tend to have better outcomes when they are in group therapies involving other patients. We also see this benefit globally. One community in eastern Africa has a village meeting at 5 a.m. to discuss dreams. They haven't reported a case of depression in over 20 years. In this way, the *human* element of medical care is coming back, but in a *digital* format. Many cultures utilize group therapy for healing.

Companies are also coming up with ways **to make networking easier and safer.** Of course, if you go online, there is also a possibility of getting false information. And reading every single patient entry to find what you are looking for won't work either. These networking companies are making efforts to moderate communities and help ensure the accuracy of information being produced. They are also developing search tools that make finding information easier and more trustable.

Patient Networks Will Unlock Health Savings

Given the rapid rise in healthcare and insurance costs, it makes sense that the medical community should tap into all the ways to improve outcomes for patients. Below are just a few companies who are making patient networking a productive experience:

- **Diabetic Connect** is part of a network of more than 50 patient-to-patient sites. Through the numerous condition-based websites, nearly 1 million patients connect, providing patient-generated information and well-being support. Patients use information from other patients on the best treatment options or services. They use moderators to make sure that any harmful information is screened out (diabeticconnect.com).

- **PatientsLikeMe** was co-founded in 2004 out of necessity. One of the founder's brothers developed ALS (Lou Gehrig's disease) at the age of 29. His family began to network with other patients around the globe. The benefits gained from this experience inspired them to build a platform for patients to share information with each other (patientslikeme.com).

- **RealSelf** is like a TripAdvisor for cosmetic procedures, where you can see thousands of reviews of various cosmetic procedures (realself.com).

- **OneHealth** (acquired by Viverae) is almost like a virtual AA program focused on drug addictions, alcoholism, eating disorders, depression, and anxiety. Their platform provides behavioral incentives and group-support techniques with the goal of building a layered intervention; it uses social solutions and peer support to keep members on target (viverae.com).

- **CaringBridge** is a non-profit that hosts websites (that anyone can start) to connect friends and families during times of need. The site was initially created in 1997 when a friend of the founder was in the middle of a high-risk pregnancy. She created the website to keep everyone informed on her friend's condition. The site also enabled everyone to communicate with each other and offer support when needed (caringbridge.org).

- **GiveForward** is an online fund raising website specifically geared toward raising money for loved ones with medical problems. Money raised can be used for medical expenses, helping patients with treatment for rare diseases, cancer, and rehabilitation. The site provides fund-raising coaches who offer ideas and guidance on how to raise money online. The site has raised over $70 million toward medical expenses (giveforward.com).

- **HealthKeep** provides anonymous and customizable health "feeds" of what people are sharing on the network, along with a database of diseases, medications, and symptoms. It connects users with others who share their health issues and addresses their privacy concerns (healthkeep.com).

- **MyHealthTeams** has created networks for chronic-condition communities to share information and stories (myhealthteams.com).

- **Crohnology** is a patient-to-patient networking and information site that collects the knowledge of others suffering from Crohn's. This is important because there are a number of strategies patients use to manage the disease in addition to taking their medications (crohnology.com).

Social Health — Gaming For Good

Employee wellness offerings now include social platforms to create successful and supportive ways to exercise and eat right. Companies are making inviting friends to participate in a 10k run and asking a buddy to go to the gym easier, more fun, and competitive. By participating in the game and exercising with your colleagues, you can win prizes or real dollars. Look to these **new technology platforms to get in shape and stay in shape.**

ShapeUp is a wellness platform that engages users in group exercises, gaming, economic incentives, and wireless technology. So let's say you have a company and you want to encourage your employees to get healthy and increase the likelihood that your team will stick to their health goals. Over the past few years, ShapeUp has shown that employees working in concert toward a goal create synergistic benefits; e.g., employees motivate other employees (shapeup.com).

Rally Health is a platform that provides monetary rewards to someone who meets their health goals. You start a group and give it a goal, like "I want to lose 20 pounds before my wedding," and followers make pledges. If you meet your goal, you get paid (rallyhealth.com).

We are just at the beginning stages of **using patients as a source to improve our system.** As we become better at extracting information from patients and making it easier for patients to share vital data, we will start to see greater benefits from the patient networking revolution. It will be easier to identify specific patients who match your specific condition and, therefore, could more effectively help you. Another patient with the same manifestation of disease as you is more likely to provide helpful information. You should consider plugging into patient networks as a routine part of managing your health.

17

SEEK TAILORED TREATMENTS

Made-for-you care should be what we expect from our system. As you know, we are not there yet. We have seen this shift in many aspects of our lives. We've evolved from using cellphones to smartphones because they have greater functionality and provide a more personalized experience. For example, you can add the apps that you want and customize the look and feel. Healthcare needs to make a similar shift—**to engage patients through a customized experience.**

All patients need to speak up and ask for more from our system. We can ask our doctors, hospital administrators, and medical researchers to look at how we can individualize care to our **unique culture, background, education, genetics, and health goals.**

This section discusses why a **customized approach** is important and even life-saving. It covers:

- How by peering into your cells we can better understand the impacts of treatments?

- Why we need to modify medical recommendations based on genetics, culture, and other factors?

- How to find medical interventions that fit your lifestyle?

- How we can improve communication between doctors and patients to overcome the medical literacy gap?

One example is a startup founder who, while attending Harvard, received a prescription for a common birth control pill to ameliorate her acne (this is quite common for young women). After she started the pill, she developed signs of depression. She went to a number of doctors, internists, and psychiatrists to understand why she had developed depression.

But her doctors, assuming it was the stress of college, put her on antidepressant medication. In fact, if you have moderate to severe signs of depression, the clinical recommendation often is to start the patient on medication. Many doctors will do this without necessarily considering that there could be another cause—it is just the way we are taught to practice. Her doctors assumed this very bright, young woman just developed a new medical condition.

She decided to dig deeper and turned to the Internet, where she found patient networking websites. She read about other patients experiencing the same depressive symptoms while on this specific birth control. She switched her birth control and her depression was gone. So in her case, her body did not process the birth control pill as most women do. And in her doctor's defense, the relationship between birth control pills and depression is not well understood. So this is the problem! For most medications, we do not clearly understand how a medication may affect a person at the cellular level.

Insider Tips

33. **Ask for the latest clinical recommendations based on your unique context.** Historically, clinical information has been based off data from a single group. If you are a minority or a woman, make sure your doctor is up-to-date on research that takes into consideration your background.

34. **Help your doctor customize your care.** Ask questions about how medical recommendations could be made specific to your unique lifestyle, diet, and health preferences.

The End Of "One Size Fits All" Care

Inadvertently, most doctors are trained and therapies are developed through a "one size fits all" approach. Doctors learn to see patterns and then make recommendations based on these patterns. Most doctors lump patients into groups this way. Drugs are developed to fit the average patient. We often don't develop drug therapies and dosages based on a patient's specific needs. You may already sense this when you get generic recommendations after you visit the ER or doctor's office.

The concern is that doctors typically only address what is in front of them and they may miss other obvious signs that aren't on their checklist. Checklists have their place; just read Atul Gawande's *The Checklist Manifesto*.

A classic example of the issues with checkbox medicine is that doctors are monitored on how often they prescribe a steroid inhaler for asthma patients. Doctors do an excellent job of prescribing

The cardiologist gave his recommendations to Sanjay and told him to stop eating steak and fatty foods. Sanjay replied, "I'm a vegetarian; I eat a lot of Indian food which has very little fat." The cardiologist sent Sanjay to see a nutritionist. Unfamiliar with the Indian diet, the nutritionist didn't know how to help him. She gave him the standard recommendation to "eat more fruits and vegetables" and "avoid saturated fats." This advice was not helpful and confusing for Sanjay. "I already eat plenty of fruits and vegetables," he thought. In the end, Sanjay went online to find a nutritionist that specialized in heart disease and had a lot of experience with numerous ethnic diets. He was given specific recipes and instructions on how to prepare foods. He felt more confident about how to optimize his heart health through modifying his diet. His healthcare became more personalized!

Many companies are working on providing more tailored experiences in some fashion. **Diabetes Plus Me** is an example of a startup aiming to create individualized treatment plans for diabetes. They have a platform that allows you to share lifestyle and medical information with your doctor and your health team (diabetesplusme.com).

Another company, **Welkin Health**, is looking to personalize care by using nurses. They have built coordination tools to pair patients with nurses to manage chronic illness (welkinhealth.com).

Tailored treatments in the long run will have a huge impact on optimizing your health. So your job is to learn if recommendations fit the uniqueness of you and to ask for more group-specific research to be done. In the next chapter, I take a deeper look into

using diagnostics in tailoring medication regiments so they can be safer and more effective.

18

THE DOCTOR WILL
SEE YOUR CELLS NOW

When I prescribe a drug, I have limited visibility into how it will truly impact the patient and affect his or her cells. This is because **medical products are designed for the average person**. I may have some general ideas of what the potential side effects are. But, as is the case for many pharma products, take Vioxx for instance, there may be unintended side effects doctors are unaware of. Vioxx was a painkiller in a similar class to ibuprofen, but it was found to increase the risk of heart attacks—this was an unexpected finding. Why would a painkiller affect the processes in the heart? Can we make taking medications safer? What should you know about taking prescription medications? As mentioned in the previous chapter getting individual therapy recommendations are critical.

We are entering an era in which doctors will be able to "see" how therapies are **affecting you at the cellular level**. As mentioned earlier, some are calling this industry initiative as **precision medicine.** They will be able to measure certain proteins within the cell and use other markers to determine how cells function. In this chapter, we will discuss how customizing therapies to your cells can make medications safer and therapies more effective. For example, it would be great to know exactly how much aspirin you need to take to lower your risk for stroke, and this way you would not be taking too much or too little.

You will need a **working knowledge** of how this new area of science can influence your body. For example, nutrigenomic analysis can be helpful in determining the best nutrition and exercise for an individual. There are already tests on the market that claim to know what diets may be best for you, given your genetic makeup.[25]

Insider Tips

35. **Ask for personalized therapies.** Find out if there are diagnostics that will tailor the need for or dose of your medications.

36. **No drug is perfect.** When we take drugs, we may have individual responses. So it is important to understand what your response may be. Sometimes minor side effects are worth the benefit that the drug provides; e.g., antibiotics cause diarrhea in some but are necessary to kill off harmful bacteria.

Taking Drugs Becomes Less Risky

Side effects—unintended adverse events on the body from taking medications—can sometimes be fatal. One of our biggest opportunities for advancement in medicine is the ability to accurately determine, ahead of time, whether a drug will be effective and have minimal side effects on an individual.

We're beginning to see progress in developing drug therapies based on genetics. The medical lingo for this is **pharmacogenetics,** an area in which genetic data is used to determine the right drug treatment for the individual. Moving forward, many therapies will include genetic analysis to determine the best treatment for you. Imagine knowing if a specific medication will work for you before treatment begins. Wouldn't this knowledge make it easier to make smarter treatment decisions or advocate for an option the doctor has not mentioned?

To make this more real, let's say you are suffering from depression and your doctor prescribes Prozac. The fact is, if you don't metabolize Prozac well, you can develop a severe headache that will make it difficult for you to want to take the medicine. At that point your doc, through sheer process of elimination, will try another antidepressant. During the **trial and error** process, unfortunately, you will still be depressed and frustrated. But if you took a blood test first to show that you were a poor metabolizer (not able to process) of certain drugs, then your doctor could start you on the right medication, saving you time and money.

Does this sound a little too futuristic? Does it take all of the uncertainty out of medicine? Absolutely not, but it can **make the trial and error approach a lot easier—smarter and faster.**

Getting The Dose Right

The ability to understand cellular pathways is helping doctors manage a number of complicated diseases. All drugs alter chemical pathways inside each person's cells to achieve a desired result. However, patients may have variations in these pathways. One might have *fast pathways* or *slow pathways* (fast and slow metabolizers, for example). Others may be missing pathways altogether. This variation greatly affects the benefits of therapy. Tests have now been developed to determine how your pathways function to improve the effectiveness of treatments.

Let's look at heart transplantation. The potential for medical complications are high. And post-transplant monitoring requires a medical procedure in which a wire is guided into your heart to get a biopsy (tissue sample) to test for rejection—every month! This is the case for heart transplant patients in the first year post-transplant. What if instead of having monthly biopsies, you could get the same rejection analysis with a blood test? **XDx** is a diagnostic company that has developed a blood test called AlloMap, which can tell if a transplanted heart is being rejected by the body without the patient enduring a risky biopsy. This way physicians can tell what is happening inside the cells to make better therapy decisions and, if rejection is seen more quickly, increase anti-rejection medications. This approach is a fraction of the cost of doing a biopsy (allomap.com).

Arthritis management is another area of disease management that is advancing quickly. Historically, rheumatologists would use a **subjective assessment** of joint pain and swelling to recommend therapy. There has not been an **objective test** to predict if a patient will undergo a painful flare-up. Moreover, this subjective assessment is compounded by the fact that the medications used to treat arthritis, like prednisone and TNF-inhibitors, are relatively potent. These therapies have significant side effects. To a certain degree, rheumatologists have been flying blind in terms of knowing when and how to prescribe these medications.

Crescendo Bioscience has developed a blood test that provides doctors with a **quantified assessment** of what is happening inside the cells of joints in rheumatology patients. This test can help doctors predict when flare-ups will occur versus the current standard of waiting for the painful symptoms to start (crescendobio.com).

As you can see, **diagnostic tests that use your body's unique chemistry** to help guide recommendations and treatments are a critical next step to making care more precise. But there's an even more sophisticated approach now available to us. By diving deeper into the cell, **into the RNA and DNA** that store our genetic code, we can unlock even more information.

Cancer Therapies Become Smarter

Traditionally, cancer treatments approached therapy in a "shotgun" manner in which healthy cells were killed along with cancer cells with hopes that the cancer cells would die more quickly. Today, new diagnostic tests can predict how well **chemotherapy will work ahead of the therapy,** as well as the likelihood that the cancer will come back. This new approach is much more targeted, instead of broad and generic.

This era of screening patients, who will achieve optimal benefit from therapies, is part of a fast moving science. We highlight a few below, but the number of companies enabling targeted cancer therapies will grow quickly.

To help doctors keep up, **Cancer IQ** is creating a database that will allow doctors to understand and keep up-to-date on which patients should get genetic testing and which ones would benefit from specific therapy (cancer-iq.com).

If you or a loved one has breast, colon, or prostate cancer and you want to find out how to optimize their treatment, **Genomic Health** is leading the path on cancer treatment optimization. Their Oncotype DX test allows doctors to better decide which chemotherapy to use for breast, colon, or prostate cancer patients. *In over 25% of cases, the test changes the recommendation that the doctor would initially have made,* in many cases avoiding a potentially harmful chemotherapy (genomichealth.com).

Pinpointing the risk of prostate cancer recurrence is also getting smarter. Traditionally, to follow the risk of recurrence of prostate cancer, doctors relied on a blood test called the PSA (prostate-specific-antigen). **GenomeDx**, using 22 genetic markers from the prostate tissue itself, developed a test that can better predict the onset of cancer recurrence because it specifically looks at protein information coming from cancer cells. This test was shown to be far more sensitive than rising PSA values (genomedx.com).

Science is now allowing doctors to understand with more precision the impact of medications on our bodies. This will make therapies safer and personalized to each patient. Patients need to understand that it is **not just about taking a pill and forgetting about it.** Patients need to be engaged with the ongoing monitoring of therapies.

Moving past cell based technologies, let's think about what could come next—a future where *no two patients* get exactly the same medical advice, or recommendations—where everything is **truly personalized to you, through digital tools.**

19

CARE GETS A MAKEOVER

s I mentioned before, doctors are short on time. In seven minutes, how is your doctor supposed to effectively cover all aspects of your lifestyle that might impact your health—sleep issues, diet, sex life, exercise? But over time, doctors will leverage body trackers, online surveys, text messaging, and other data collection tools **outside of the visit** to provide customized recommendations. In the previous chapter, we discussed diagnostics driving customization, now we explore other digital tools that help do the same.

Physicians who are engaging patients with these types of apps could make appropriate modifications to their treatment plan according to the data presented by the patient. Similarly, patients would be more likely to adhere to their treatment plans because they would understand that it was more tailored to them.

For example, doctors could prescribe a web-enabled weight scale and blood pressure monitor and receive a weekly summary of weight, blood pressure, and other measurements. If a new blood pressure medication is prescribed, the effects on hypertension can be easily and more routinely monitored at home.

Imagine receiving precise information on when to take medications that suits your body. The doctor can also tailor the medication dosage and timing—**is the morning or the evening a better time to take your blood pressure medications?** For some hypertensive patients, their blood pressure is higher in the AM than PM, so knowing this, the doctor can more accurately tell a patient when to take their medications. Unfortunately, most doctors don't have this very patient-specific information at the time of prescribing.

Therapies Get Lifestyle-Centric

With patient-specific data feeds, physicians can much more easily tailor recommendations. A few companies are listed below to show examples of these platforms:

- **WellApps** enables patients to follow symptoms and allows physicians to have detailed reports. Patients also have a better understanding of how taking—or skipping—their medicine impacts their condition (wellapps.com).

- **Symple** allows you to track symptoms in a diary-type fashion. Catalog symptoms and rate how intense they were. The symptom data is then interpreted and compiled, and a report is created that is shared with your doctor (sympleapp.com).

- **MyPictureRx** is a medication management tool that uses pictures to explain what you are taking, how to take it, and why you are taking a specific medication. They also send you a reminder when you are due for a refill (mypicturerx. com).

- **ChickRX** is an online community designed for women. Users can ask questions of other members or wellness experts. It's more like reading a magazine than looking at a medical website, so it makes reading about health fun (chickrx.com).

- **Care at Hand** is a platform that allows home health aides to become better equipped at identifying and reporting concerns. This provides a better feedback loop for physicians and family members (careathand.com).

Everybody Knows Your Name

We all know how a personal touch makes us feel. It's a Saturday morning when my wife and I go to Starbucks and the barista knows our name and the order. It's the little things, but they leave a great impression.

Personalization is necessary in all facets of healthcare, not just for therapies. It's like having your name on a medical handout; it's talking to you at your literacy level; it's knowing who is on your medical team. As we age as a country, more people need healthcare services, and there will be a growing need for all parts of the system to become more engaged and individualized—or risk becoming cold and impersonal.

Insider Tips

37. Research digitals tools that can make **your care more individualized**. It is also important to loop in, and potentially train, your doctor on these new tools.

> 38. **Hack your meds.** Most of us hate taking pills (or forget)—
> try **technology that takes the drudgery** out taking
> medications.

Below are some companies creating more tailored health experiences:

- **Avva Advocate** helps breast cancer patients navigate diagnosis, treatment and survivorship. The company works with each patient to develop a list of questions to discuss with their doctor based on their personal situation, symptoms, and latest developments (avvahealth.com).

- **Avado** is a patient-relationship management site that was bought by WebMD. They provide you with an online account that houses all of your records and conversations with your care team and physicians (webmd.com).

- **Visible Health Connect** is another platform that enables patients and physicians to securely share health charts and treatment options (visiblehealth.com).

- **Abiogenix** has created uBox, **a wireless pillbox** and web portal to increase medication adherence. It can alert you when to take your meds and will text or email your family if you forgot so they can remind you as well (abiogenix.com).

On a side note, insurance companies are moving from just handling the financial transactions to really managing health and creating more value for every dollar spent on a health plan. Personalization is still in the early days, but it is what most payers are focused on.

Your Pillbox Gets A Glow-Over!

Patients hate taking pills. Older patients who have to take 20 to 30 pills can find this process hard to manage or remember to do each day. A solution is here—**GlowCaps**, a product introduced by the company **Vitality,** uses technology to remind people to take their medications through visual and auditory reminders. Imagine a glowing electronic pill-bottle cap that communicates with your phone, reminding you to take your pills or get a refill.

The reminder process is simple. First, the cap will alert you with blinking lights, and then, should the visual reminder fail, a ringtone will sound. If these reminders don't work, the cap will send a text to a family member, alerting them that you forgot to take the pill. The user's adherence is monitored and a report is sent to their doctor, which introduces accountability into the equation. Now that the patient feels more accountable, it is more likely they will take the medication as directed.

Healthcare is going through a **magnificent transformation** as it tries to make **each person feel unique**—from the little step of knowing which pharmacy you prefer to creating information that you can read and that makes sense to you. Over the next few years expect to see your hospital and doctor offer more custom services because it just makes sense.

But we also know that most medical information is difficult to comprehend, and who remembers what a doctor tells them in detail? In the next section, I talk about how "health talk" must become more personalized. We spend trillions but a lot of this is wasted because patients don't fully understand what their doctors are saying.

20

SIRI, WHAT DID MY DOCTOR SAY?

We all forget what the doctor says…or we can't really understand what we do remember. As I mentioned, when you leave a doctor's office or ER, you are given a generic, pre-fabricated form discussing your health problems. Doctors usually provide a quick one to two minute discussion around these instructions, but many doctors have canned, rehearsed communication that they recite regarding hypertension, diabetes, etc. Very little is customized to a person's culture, socioeconomic background, lifestyle, or personality type. Doctors just don't have the time and may not have the incentives to truly provide individualized care.

Doctors need to understand their patients in order to really get the message across. For example, some patients need a lot of details and explanation before they'll buy-in and follow through with instructions. Other patients just want to know the basic next steps without getting buried with too much information. There's growing evidence that patients' preset attitudes will ultimately drive adoption and compliance of their therapies. Moreover, if you don't *feel* like a doctor's instructions apply to you, you're less likely to follow those instructions. Therefore, it is crucial for healthcare to understand people, their attitudes and perceptions, and how to impact their behaviors in effective ways.

> **Insider Tip**
>
> 39. **Using tools to remember what the doctor says** could be the easiest way to improve your health. We lose a lot of medical value if we don't remember recommendations.

Communication Gets Personal

To illustrate why communication is so important, let me tell you a story. While working in the ER, I had a patient who had upper abdominal pain. She had an abnormal ultrasound of her gallbladder and so I called the on call surgeon. He came to see the patient and said, "You need a choley" (medical shorthand for cholecystectomy or gallbladder removal surgery), and took the patient to surgery.

The patient had the surgery and two days later came back to the ER for the same abdominal pain. After speaking with her for a while, I asked if she knew what procedure she had and she replied, "a choley." I then asked her if she knew where her gallbladder was and she pointed to her belly button where the surgery scar was. The gallbladder is actually located on the upper right side of the abdomen. So this patient had an entire surgery done and had no clue where her gallbladder was located! She did not know that she might have some pain in that area after surgery and made an unnecessary trip to the ER.

As doctors, we are aware that patients come from different educational backgrounds, yet most of us don't tailor our communication.

As a medical community, we have **done a poor job of educating people about their own bodies**—this is one reason why medical costs are on the rise. Solutions to address this have been difficult to implement in the past. With advancements in technology, like handheld iPads, it is now an attainable goal.

Emmi Solutions is a company focused on improving the educational process for surgical procedures and other health events that a patient goes through, by creating easy-to-understand information about risks and benefits of surgery (emmisolutions. com).

Sometimes the problem is that the doctor and patient just don't speak the same language. In person translators aren't always available, but new solutions to address this communication barrier are emerging.

Numerous companies are tackling this issue, but of note two medical students at UCSF created a *free* medical translation app. **MediBabble** serves as a professional grade medical translation tool between a patient and their doctor when there is a language barrier (medibabble.com).

Even when physicians and patients speak the same language, communication needs to be tailored to fit each patient's comprehension level. This could be as simple as cutting out medical jargon or changing communication formats; e.g., incorporating apps and using visual aids or podcasts. Researchers estimate that patients only remember 15% of things they were told in the doctor's office. Providing them with relevant reminders and other such information in language they can understand will greatly increase their adherence to recommendations.

A lot of people, for example, are diagnosed with high blood pressure and instructed to take medications on a daily basis. However, many of them don't know what high blood pressure is, nor do they understand the full impact of this disease. Data shows that only 20-50% of all medications are taken by patients.[26] This is a waste of their money and, more importantly, dangerous to their health. Improving compliance through better communication and monitoring platforms could lead to dramatic savings.

Below are some companies trying to help improve how patients follow medical recommendations:

- **HealthVoice App** allows you to securely record your doctor's recommendations and share them with your care team. Share what one doctor says with another doctor, improving coordination and streamlining care (healthvoiceapp.com).

- **Voxiva** has a very successful Text4baby program that promotes good health practices among pregnant women. It works by sending instant messages via your phone, reminding pregnant women about engaging in healthy behaviors (text4baby.org).

- **HealthCrowd** combines text messaging with behavioral change and uses specific timing of those messages when patients are most likely to take action with regards to medications and other health measures (healthcrowd.com).

- **DrawMD** offers customizable anatomy slides. A physician can draw on and use this visual aid to explain complex procedures and break down communication barriers for patients (drawmd.com).

In the future, tailored transactions will also allow information to be **delivered based on the patient's preferences, ethnicity, gender, and primary language.** As a result, we're going to see much more tailored communication between patients and health systems, insurers, and medical professionals. Patients will be given the option to choose the type of communication they prefer. Some may want videos; others, text messaging. I believe, this **customization will improve patient compliance, adoption, understanding,** and most importantly, help to save lives.

It is critical for the medical community **to get this right**—otherwise, we will continue throwing money down this communication gap.

21

COMPLEMENT YOUR CARE

Traditional doctors are in short supply. Smart Patients must complement their healthcare with other models of care. Moreover, there is evidence to show that alternative care is quite effective. You will also need to understand how to best utilize mid-level providers who are taking on more care activities within the system.

When is it okay to see a nurse practioner (NP) in a pharmacy clinic? What ailments should I see a naturopath for? What can a dietician help me with? These are all questions that Smart Patients need to start asking.

Alternative and complementary therapy models are acupuncture, chiropractic care, naturopathic medicine, and energy healing, just to name a few. These non-traditional therapies are continuing to show great progress and are integrating into the traditional medical framework. Given the growing evidence and future importance of these complementary health approaches, I thought it would be important to include them in this book.

> **Insider Tips**
>
> 40. **Over time research will continue to validate the value of complementary care.** Given that it is now easier than ever to find a well-reviewed naturopath or acupuncturist—it is a great time to see if these care models can help you with migraines, back pain, asthma, diabetes, etc.
>
> 41. **Mid-level providers are becoming increasingly integrated into the medical landscape.** It is important to understand when and how to best utilize their services—because they are often easier to get appointments with and lower in cost than physician providers.

Rent-A-Guru—Alternative Providers Fuel Feeling Better

Although some doctors have differing views on the benefits of alternative medicine, I truly believe it can help you recover faster. It also can work hand-in-hand with traditional Western medicine. For example, you can take medications to lower your blood pressure; but by doing acupuncture in conjunction with medication, the benefit can be greater.[27] Therefore alternative medicine can bring down the overall cost of care compared to just using traditional approaches.

Alternative medicine is difficult to define but includes energy healing, meditation, herbal remedies, acupuncture, massage, etc. For some patients, these **therapies can work better for some illnesses than traditional medicine**. Patients suffering from chronic pain, cancer care, allergies, depression, and other conditions find real value in these therapies. I believe that alternative care will eventually blend seamlessly with traditional care. Moreover, **many alternative therapies are going digital**—for example, you can do live yoga or meditation sessions on a platform called **Learn It Live** (LearnItLive.com). Overtime, more alternative practices will be available online, in hand-held devices, and via smartphones; it will be important to be tuned into any future developments in this space.

Alternative practices can also help alleviate stress from work, family, and other responsibilities that can have a deleterious effect on your health. Studies have shown that stress can cause a myriad of physical and mental symptoms. But instead of waiting until you've developed aches and pains and have started taking medications, you could make a much smaller investment in yoga, acupuncture, or massage. A membership to a hot yoga studio (Bikram) is exceedingly cheaper than the cost of psychotherapy.

Wellness apps for your phone are popping up everywhere. In fact, the wellness and alternative industry's growth is exploding and is estimated to be nearly a trillion dollar market.[28] People are spending big dollars to incorporate alternative health practitioners like naturopaths, acupuncturists, nutritionists, massage therapists, and many other non-traditional health providers into their care.

New digital companies are reshaping how we engage with alternative care, and these resources can speed up your care. Below are only a few that are already available:

Meditation

Meditation has been touted as benefiting you by reducing stress, anxiety, and depression—improving focus—and even boosting your immune system. New research shows that meditation may actually change your brain for the better, help with mild cognitive impairment, and reduce pain and migraine headaches, so what are you waiting for? Turn on your inner "om." Below are a few companies that can help you:

- **MindBody** has created a marketplace for employees to access non-traditional providers (mindbodyonline.com).

- **Mindfulness** allows you to meditate to music or relax through a voice-guided meditation. You choose the length and you can even set a reminder to alert you when it's time to practice (mindapps.se).

- **My Headspace** adapts to your mindfulness and meditation practice for an on-the-go lifestyle (getsomeheadspace.com).

- **Buddhify** provides bite-size guided meditation sessions on the go. It offers a modern approach to meditation while also retaining the depth of practice from years of combined meditation experience (buddhify.com).

- **DoYogaWithMe** is an online platform that offers an easy-to-follow beginners guide. You get two classes and one pose tutorial each week. Browse classes by difficulty, length, style, and teacher. Also see video ratings and reviews from your fellow yogis (doyogawithme.com).

- **Chakra Balancing and Energy Healing** helps you sense, activate, and balance your energy through a voice-guided session, so you can start healing from the inside out (meditationoasis.com).

- **Learn It Live** has numerous wellness, meditation, and yoga classes that you can participate in from the comfort of your home (learnitlive.com).

Optimize Your Healing Through Food

Companies are popping up to help you eat better by taking all the guesswork out of what is good for you. Most of these companies work closely with nutritionists to review their content and product offerings:

- **Zipongo** is a mobile platform that promotes healthy eating by understanding your food preferences and food sale items. This helps you create recipes and personalize meal plans based on your taste and what's on sale at your local grocery store (zipongo.com).

- **Oh My Green** (Omg) provides food with benefits. They have an online and mobile wellness platform that offers products that are organic, non-GMO, taste tested, and nutritionist verified (ohmygreen.com).

Benefits of Complementary Care

Cancer Treatment Centers of America is integrating services such as nutrition therapy, naturopathic medicine, chiropractic care, and mind-body and spiritual support in conjunction with traditional cancer treatments. Cancer care is important to all of us because we all know someone who has been affected by this disease. There have been numerous clinical studies showing that alternative practices like meditation and energy healing can improve outcomes and reduce the pain associated with cancer.

Organizations like Kaiser Permanente, a multibillion-dollar health delivery company, have been covering integrative and complementary medicine, including practices like chiropractic care, massage, acupuncture, nutritional support, and mind-body classes, to help promote a greater sense of emotional, physical, and spiritual well-being.

Mid-Level Providers Take Center Stage

Mid-level providers (MLPs) are medical workers who have titles like physician assistants (PAs) or nurse practitioners (NPs). All mid-level providers are supervised and trained by doctors.

Although both PAs and NPs have been around for nearly 30 years, only in the last decade have we seen an increase in the number of these providers. According to the American Academy of Physician Assistants and the American Academy of Nurse Practitioners, 221,000 mid-level providers currently work in the US. This is more than a 100% increase from the estimated 103,612 employed just 10 years ago.

Along with this growth has come better training, which has led to better quality care and expanded utilization of MLPs. Mid-level providers can do an excellent job of providing care or implementing the recommendations from the doctor for about 80% of primary care problems. For example, if you need sutures, or treatment for a UTI, sore throat, or a headache, an MLP can handle the job.

Don't be reluctant to seek these providers, especially when doing so may provide a faster resolution for your medical concerns. **Novel approaches are emerging that will provide "software" supervision to make sure MLPs** are providing the right care and triaging to a doctor when necessary. For example, **GuideVue** has developed an iPhone application that enables nurses, among other things, to evaluate the eye in the same way that an ophthalmologist would, through a real time, guided process. Nurses are using this tool to determine which patients have high-priority eye disease. It also intelligently sorts which patients need an emergency consultation with an eye surgeon. GuideVue is also used by the Department of Defense to help non-clinically trained soldiers perform first aid and minor procedures. These types of technologies, developed for non-medical personnel, could help MLPs (and physicians for that matter).

Overall, I think it is important to **know how and when to use non-physician providers.** As I mentioned, it may be increasingly difficult to get all your care needs met from just one medical provider. I also believe it is important for you to have a game plan as it relates to non-traditional healthcare—from energy healing, meditation, acupuncture, massage, and yoga. More of these therapies will also make their way into your smartphones, iPads, and computers, making them easy to access.

Personal Trainer Meets Acupuncturist

Mike is a personal trainer who is a relatively active individual. He "threw out his back" at the gym while lifting heavy weights showing off to some of his friends. Years of heavy weight training caused some serious inflammation.

His pain was so severe that he could barely walk straight. He visits his doctor, who prescribes some pills that do not help. On his next visit he gets a shot. The pain continues; Mike tries hot and cold therapies, but nothing is working. Frustrated with the constant pain, he remembers that one of his clients is actually a certified acupuncturist; Mike decides to call him and starts his acupuncture therapy. After weeks of regular sessions, Mike is pain free and enjoying training his clients again.

22

CARE TAKES FLIGHT

When my mom visits India, I make her get a complete set of diagnostics—it's cheap, safe, fast, and there are no squabbles with insurance. Although it sounds humorous, getting screened this way in India is very affordable, e.g., about $100 for an MRI. In fact, services there are so much cheaper and easier to access that it makes the expense and trouble of traveling worth it.

As a Smart Patient, you may need to travel abroad to get a better bang for your buck. This industry, known as **medical tourism**, is rapidly becoming a way to get legitimate care at lower costs. The consulting firm Deloitte and Touché has estimated that the medical tourism market is worth $333 million.[29] Currently, this industry mainly focuses on **orthopedic, dental, plastic, and cardiovascular surgery** located in Latin America and Asia. These countries are

181

recruiting patients from the US, where the costs of similar services can be 10-20x higher. In the rest of the world, traveling abroad for medical care has become relatively common. The UK government, for example, where cardiac bypass patients wait 2 to 6 months or more for surgeries, is considering sending those patients abroad.[30]

Numerous companies offer **full concierge experiences for travel abroad** medical procedures. These services will help you arrange the entire process, from visas, tickets, hotels, transfers, and post-procedure rehab, to making sure you have the right food and pleasant local cultural experiences. They typically have negotiated rates with hospitals, doctors, and hotels, and smooth the transit process of transfers and getting around. They also assist with any issues that may arise during the trip—so all in all, a helpful service, unless you are like Anthony Bourdain of CNN and can parachute into any country. Knowing the importance of customer service and better outcomes for sustaining future business, they typically give you a royal treatment during your stay!

Digital technologies are **creating the bridge to other countries**. With technologies like Skype and the fact that English has become the *de facto* global language in healthcare, it has become a lot easier to get familiar with **surgical options as well as get a virtual tour of each facility.**

Most health organizations competing for medical tourism customers are adopting international standards, so you can expect a high standard of care within these countries. Medical destinations are also getting accredited. **The Joint Commission,** which accredits US health organizations, has rapidly increased its efforts to provide international accreditation, and now many Indian and Latin American hospitals are accredited to international standards.

Some employers are also jumping on board. In an effort to lower costs, numerous US employers are subsidizing the cost of travel to help employees get care abroad, which brings cost savings to the employer. You should check with your HR department—many of them are now considering this path to lowering costs.

Insider Tip

42. Medical tourism is a viable **way to save money**. Moreover, international quality and safety standards are quickly emerging, making the quality of services similar across countries. Also, choose medical tourism providers that **allow you to speak with other patients** who have used their services.

Here is a partial list of companies specializing in these services:

- **MedToGo.com** is an online company that has been arranging medical tourism visits to Mexico since 2000. Surgeons are also thoroughly reviewed by the organization.

- **Planet Hospital** allows you to choose from a list of procedures, treatments, and surgeons across countries. It also shows the estimated hospitalization costs (planethospital.com).

- **MedRetreat** offers surgical procedures in Brazil, Argentina, or Thailand for 80% less than what they cost in the US. They offer a guarantee to all patients: If you arrive at your destination country and the conditions are not acceptable to you, you have the option to cancel your surgery without any financial obligation (medretreat.com).

- **Patients Beyond Borders** is a company that offers comprehensive services in medical tourism outlining how to determine if medical travel is right for you, how to find the best hospitals and clinics around the world, and how to plan and budget for your trip (patientsbeyondborders.com).

- **MedicalTourism.com** is a free, confidential, independent resource for patients and industry providers.

The Value Of Having Surgery Abroad

Brad, who is 57, ran a lot in high school and college. Even today he's still very active. He's still young, but he's starting to show signs of osteoarthritis. His doctors have told him he'll need a knee replacement to keep up with his active lifestyle pain-free. He has insurance and his provider mentioned that they will actually cover more of the cost of the surgical procedure if it's done in Thailand. Brad has never been to Thailand; he's intrigued, but a little nervous. The program would include knee replacement surgery and three weeks of rehab in a hospital in Thailand. He has questions about his procedure, so he goes online and is able to Skype with the doctor who will perform his surgery.

He's impressed with the doctor and he would love a vacation, so he tells his insurance company that he's ready to go to Thailand. The insurance company introduces Brad to a medical- travel company that acts as a concierge service for him: They pick him up at the airport, arrange for his stay, and coordinate surgery and rehabilitation services. He has a restful and enjoyable experience in Thailand and comes away spending $2,000 less than he would have if he had stayed home for the surgery.

Over time, many experts believe that surgical standardization will provide patients more options and lower-cost ways of getting the care they need abroad. Digital tools and websites will play an important role in connecting US patients and doctors abroad. For this reason, I thought it was important to include a chapter on this category of health services. It may be helpful for some patients.

23

CONNECTED DOCTORS HEAL THE SYSTEM

Many doctors have stopped doctoring. They don't have time. It is hard for our country to overnight produce top-notch doctors, so we need to do more with the current pool of doctors. [31] One solution is to equip physicians with digital tools that can aid them to more fully engage patients—and, to one end, help them doctor again. The **end result of retooling doctors will be truly optimized care** for you. It will be critical for Smart Patients to encourage physicians and health systems to go digital and is the reason why it's highlighted in the book. Moreover, this improvement in physician productivity will be needed for the ACA to work.

Today, doctors can upload informational videos into the Cloud, post messages and health campaigns on Facebook, and overall engage patients on platforms that they are already using and are familiar with. However, only a few are doing this. **Making digital technology work for doctors** will be critical to making this transformation succeed. We have to make it super easy for them and provide reimbursement for their digital activity.

The problem is, doctors don't learn about this approach in medical school. And as a physician, I can say that doctors in general are slow to adopt new technologies, so it is important for innovation teams within health organizations to help resolve this issue.

Moreover, **better networking among doctors will lead to better and cheaper care.** In the ER, when I admit a patient for signs of a stroke, I call a neurologist, who will often order an MRI for the next day. Since they are trying to make good use of their time and because they don't know when the MRI will be completed, the neurologist usually waits until the end of the day to see those patients. But the anxious patient and their loved ones have no idea when the neurologist will come in to see them. To make it easier on patients and families, could we have iPads in patient rooms that show them when a doctor will arrive, and update the arrival time during the day (similar to Uber)? Given the speed at which technology has become part of our daily lives, there must be ways to make care collaboration faster and better because this will significantly drive down care costs.

Insider Tips

43. **Doctors are learning to go social and mobile,** and this will transform how you engage with them. Be prepared for this change.

44. **Choose health systems that invest heavily in helping doctors deliver better care.** Health systems will kick-start physician connectedness to improve physician decision-making and patient care. Interview your local hospital to find out what digital services they are offering.

Physicians Go Digital To Doctor Again

Social media, mobilization of delivery, and the ability to provide localized information (like the price of a CT) are the key focus areas for technological advancements.

Physicians are also becoming accessible 24/7 through video chats and other interactive platforms. Doctors can provide tutorials, webinars, and videos to educate patients. One doctor uses videos to teach new mothers the ins and outs of breastfeeding. Another offers videos to educate family members on how to care for someone after cataract surgery. It is a great way to educate not only the patient, but anyone involved in caregiving.

Digital doctoring will have profound effects on improving patient compliance. The networked doctor will create a following, provide better care, and spur other physicians to offer similar services for their patients.

It will also enable physicians to create "brands" around their services. One emerging trend is that doctors are developing their own apps—"the Dr. Smith app"—to connect directly with their patients via smartphones. With their own apps, doctors can provide precise recommendations and offer a collection of their favorite go-to health sites. If your doctor doesn't have an app, you might want to encourage them to get one.

For example, **Fibroblast** makes referrals after a doctor's visit easier because it allows for scheduling right away. When you are referred, instead of calling the specialist's office, you can schedule right from the primary care office (fibroblast.com).

Bridging The Doctor Shortage

Physicians networking with other providers will be one of the keys to addressing physician shortages in parts of the US and around the world. Networked physicians will also be able to improve productivity by coordinating care better and having the right doctor take care of the right problem. Doctors can provide quicker consults by taking a photo of an EKG and sending it to a cardiologist, for example, or taking a photo of a rash and sending it to a dermatologist. The following companies are helping to coordinate care:

- **TigerText** is making it easy for doctors in the same hospital to chat and coordinate patient care (tigertext.com).

- **Doximity** is building a LinkedIn-type network for physicians (doximity.com).

- **Sermo** allows doctors to privately discuss cases with other doctors (sermo.com).

- **AgileMD** helps doctors make guided decisions by connecting them to the most up-to-date information all within a patient visit. They estimate that 1 in 7 patients are misdiagnosed. So having this type of technology during the patient visit can lower the error rate (agilemd.com).

- **QuantiaMD** is a networking site for physicians where they can ask questions of each other (quantiamd.com).

- **Docphin** allows doctors to check in with a number of medical information sources in one location. It will also send personal recommendations from the news, journals, and even Twitter (docphin.com).

On a slightly different note, **Truth On Call** hopes to provide critical connections between medical providers in developing countries with those in the developed world through an extensive network of connected physicians. It allows doctors to quickly poll other physicians and receive guidance (truthoncall.com).

Technology has and will continue to revolutionize "doctoring." New platforms will emerge that connect doctors, care teams, and patients, and this virtual provider team will take care of you, regardless of your location. This is the exciting future of healthcare—as more **doctors use networking in the practice of caring for patients.**

24

DIGITAL HEALTH IN ACTION

A s I mentioned in the subtitle, we are just at the beginning of the digital era of medicine. It is a **powerful new opportunity to transform our system**—and in this chapter I want to take mini dives into specific conditions so that readers with specific issues may benefit. Each of the conditions could have its own chapter but I am only providing a snapshot to provide a flavor of how you can use digital technologies for them.

But let's start with a story demonstrating digital health in action and grounding us to where the union of technology and medicine can take us. Let's imagine that John, who is 37, works for an international company and lives in three cities during the year: London, Chicago, and Singapore. He is also diabetic and is committed to taking care of his health. Given his travel, it is practically impossible for him to make doctor's appointments. So instead John finds a doctor who has a virtual practice in addition to a brick-and-mortar one—Dr. Shah.

John also believes in educating himself, and he religiously spends his Tuesday mornings reading up on the latest information related to diabetes, nutrition, and wellness. John has a text messaging plan with his doctor that allows him to send and receive secure messages. Every three months, John visits his doctor virtually for a 30-minute session. He also makes a yearly visit in person to see his doctor to get a physical. John carries a device that monitors his blood sugar and vital signs and sends alerts to his doctor if there are abnormalities.

At his office, Dr. Shah has a futuristic device that uses John's scanned measurements and creates a 3-D full inside-and-out body blueprint. It records his vitals, heart sounds, breath sounds, and internal imaging. With his 3-D model, if John has to ever see another doctor, that doctor can see what John's baseline examination was. John can access this when needed, which is especially helpful in emergencies. John doesn't have to wait for reports to be generated and sent; this 3-D image gives any new doctor a lot faster access to information.

John developed a bad and unusual headache while he was in Singapore. He went to the local ER, where he was able to show the ER doc his 3-D model. The doctor noticed that John had an anomaly in his blood vessels that might cause him to have a brain aneurysm. The ER doc quickly got a CT angiogram of his head, which showed he did have an aneurysm. Luckily for John, it was caught in time and fixed before it became an issue.

As you can see, healthcare can be a lot different. Over time we will get there, but we will get there sooner as more patients ask for these changes.

Digital Health Examples By Condition

This section lays out more recommendations based on specific health conditions or interests. This is not an exhaustive list. And I am not trying to endorse any specific company but just providing an illustrative snapshot of each condition. Some conditions, like diabetes and heart disease, deserve their own digital book. Please do your own research to see what's out there—most of it can be found on the Internet.

We will cover the following conditions and how to make them faster, better, smarter, and cheaper for you.

1. Pregnancy
2. For Babies
3. Nutrition
4. Diabetes
5. Sleep Better
6. Heart Health
7. General Health & Wellness
8. Sexual Health
9. Seizure Care
10. Asthma
11. Depression
12. Skin Cancer
13. Weight Loss

PREGNANCY

The good news is that there are tons of apps that can help you with your pregnancy. They can tell you the best days to try to conceive. Once you have conceived, then you can consider the health of your baby and how to best maintain your own health throughout your pregnancy. For example, do you need to be taking folate more than other women to guard against genetic defects? Also make sure that you find the best value for your care through site comparisons of price and quality. Here are a few suggestions of technology that will help you get pregnant, have a healthy pregnancy, and have a smooth delivery:

1. **First, get pregnant.**
   - **Ovuline** follows your menstrual cycle and makes customized predictions about your ovulation and fertile window (ovuline.com).
   - **VitaPath Genetics** offers a screening test that tells you if you need to be taking folate, which helps prevent spina bifida (alere.com).
   - **Panorama** prenatal test provides non-invasive genetic screening for gender and several serious genetic disorders such as Down syndrome; you can get tested as early as nine weeks (panoramatest.com).

2. **Have a healthy pregnancy.**
   - **Voxiva's Text4Baby** sends text messages tailored to individual cultures and languages, reminding pregnant women about engaging in healthy behaviors (text4baby. org).
   - **Mobile Mom** tracks your due date once you're pregnant, your weight throughout pregnancy, and your baby's kicks with a kick counter (mobilemom.com).
   - With **Sprout Baby**, you can see your baby's development in real time. Sprout also includes doctors' recommendations, health tips, a weight tracker tool, a visit planner, and a contraction timer (medart-studios.com).

3. **Have a better delivery.**
   - **A contraction timer** is a helpful feature offered by several apps that can clear up confusion on the timing

between contractions and when you may need to head to the hospital (contractionmaster.com).

- **Sense4Baby** continuously and wirelessly monitors the baby's heart rate for signs of fetal distress for those mothers and babies that may need it (airstrip.com).

FOR BABIES

Every parent wants to optimize their baby's health and be in tune with their baby's habits. Thankfully, there are many apps dedicated to do just that. Some monitor for signs of illness or risk of developing disease. Others help you learn how to anticipate your baby's needs by learning their unique "schedule."

There are also smart monitoring technologies that will help you rest easy knowing you have access to your baby. Here's a good place to start:

1. **Ensure your baby's health is optimal.**
   - **Trixie Tracker** stores your baby's activities, including sleeping, feeding, diaper changes, new foods, and medications (trixietracker.com).
   - **BabyBix** tracks your baby's sleep, diaper changes, feeding patterns, and growth (babybix.com).
   - **LatchMD** is a great resource to learn about the best techniques to manage and succeed with breastfeeding (latchmd.com).
   - **Pixie Scientific's Smart Diapers** monitor for urinary tract infections, prolonged dehydration, and chronic kidney conditions (pixiescientific.com).
   - For infants with a temperature, some parents may want to try **e-Skin** by Vivalink which makes it possible for parents to measure their children's body temperature

via a thin, flexible adhesive bandage that sends an electronic reading to their smartphone (vivalnk.com/ eskin-thermometer).

2. **Ensure your baby is sleeping soundly.**
   - **Withings Smart Baby Monitor** allows for constant monitoring of your baby with sound as well as video input. It also allows for two-way communication or music to start remotely (withings.com).

NUTRITION

There are an abundance of apps that focus on nutrition, ranging from those that are purely educational to those that offer recipes and weight loss strategies. Learn about what is in your food, how it measures against other foods, and how to make better choices. Put this knowledge to use and build healthier meals. Some also have the ability to warn you when a food you've chosen contains a harmful allergen. Some technologies go a step beyond and will build a diet specifically with you in mind, using personal data such as blood work and body type for optimization. It's difficult to sort the good from the not so useful, but here are some great examples to follow:

1. **Get smarter about what is in your food.**
   - **Fooducate** shows detailed nutritional information once an item's UPC code is scanned (fooducate.com).
   - **GoodGuide** provides rankings of foods and other products based on whether they're safe, healthy, green, and socially responsible (goodguide.com).
   - Input your grocery list and **Shopwell** gives you an overall health "score" for each item. Set up a profile that includes food allergies, foods you'd like to avoid,

and your nutrition goals, and shop based on these specifications (shopwell.com).

2. **Use what you learned to plan better meals.**

- **Zipongo** helps you plan your meal and also save money by helping you find low cost healthy food (zipongo.com).

- **Mobile Food Coach** allows you to upload photos of meals and connect with certified nutrition coaches to make sure you're making healthy food choices (mobilefoodcoach.com).

3. **Avoid ingredients you're allergic to.**

- **Allergy Caddy** includes information on the top 10 allergens/sensitivities and data for 40 fast food restaurants (allergycaddy.com).

- **Foods You Can** lets you scan and identify foods you are allergic to so you can avoid them (foodsyoucan.com).

- **MyFoodFacts** helps you identify foods with allergens and gives you critical information on food product recalls (myfoodfacts.com).

- **Grain or No Grain** allows you to test your gluten knowledge by taking a quiz, learning about safe and unsafe foods, and reviewing which restaurant menu items are gluten-free (grainornograin.com).

DIABETES

Diabetes management has greatly benefited from the advent of care coordination tools and innovative diagnostics. Imagine knowing your risk of developing diabetes—so you can start preventing it today. Or imagine an easy-to-use platform to manage your medications and recording your blood sugars that goes directly to your doctor. Diabetics can also network with other diabetics to make better lifestyle choices and have automated insulin delivery.

Technologies also exist that will alert patients if complications such as a foot ulcer or low blood sugar are developing in order to avert further consequences.

1. **Assess your risk for diabetes.**
   - **Omada Health** uses a group coaching model to help reduce the risk of diabetes in pre-diabetics (preventnow. com).
   - **Prognomix** is currently developing four tests that will predict the likelihood you will get diabetes (prognomix.com).

2. **Measure and track your blood glucose on the go.**
   - **Glucose Buddy** helps store data for people with diabetes. You manually enter your glucose numbers, carbohydrate consumption, insulin dosages, and activities. Then view and share that data with your doctor for better diabetes management (glucosebuddy. com).
   - **Glooko** allows readings from a patient's glucometer to be logged in an app. It also records food choices, medication, and exercise (glooko.com).
   - **Dexcom** has created a continuous glucose monitoring device. The small sensor enables you to get real time readings throughout the day, which helps you become smarter about your diabetes management (dexcom.com).
   - **WellDoc** monitors blood sugar and helps prevent a hypoglycemic episode by sending alerts (welldoc.com).

- **CareLogger** helps people with diabetes measure and follow their glucose levels, blood pressure, meals, and weight (carelogger.com).

3. **Optimize your insulin delivery.**
   - **Cellnovo** has a technology that integrates blood glucose and activity monitors, diet trackers, and insulin pumps, which provides a holistic approach to managing diabetes (cellnovo.com).

4. **Manage diabetic complications better.**
   - **Orpyx's** shoe inserts can detect the early stages of a foot ulcer (orphyx.com).

SLEEP BETTER

Getting a good night's sleep is important to your overall health. Some apps are attempting to help patients learn about their sleep cycle: what makes their sleep better (more restful) and worse. This information can be used to give you a better night's sleep. Some sleep cycle apps even integrate an alarm to gently wake you up during your lightest phase of sleep.

There are also technologies that can remotely monitor patients for sleep apnea, a difficult-to-diagnose sleep disorder that is associated with a host of chronic medical problems.

1. **Track your sleep cycle and collect data.**
   - **SleepBot** is a sleep cycle tracker that allows you to record movements throughout the night (mysleepbot.com).
   - **SleepCycle** tracks your sleep patterns and wakes you up in your lightest sleep phase (sleepcycle.com).

2. **Check yourself for sleep apnea (30 million Americans are undiagnosed).**

- **Novasom** makes a home sleep apnea sensor called AccuSom. It means that you can wear a portable sleep sensor at home instead of staying in an unfamiliar place where sleeping may be difficult (novasom.com).
- **Clevemed** makes Sleepview, which is another wearable home monitoring device to help detect sleep apnea (clevemed.com).

HEART HEALTH

Cardiovascular disease is one of the leading causes of death in America. The list below is one approach to improving your heart health with digital tools.

So far, technologies exist that allow easy-to-use remote heart monitoring and new diagnostics that will predict your risk of having a heart attack in the future.

1. **Monitor your heart.**
   - **Zio Patch** is a Band-Aid-sized heart monitor that can be worn under your clothes (irhythmtech.com).
   - **AliveCor** attaches to your mobile device to capture an EKG and send it to your doctor (alivecor.com).
   - **Azumio** has apps for testing stress, improving workouts, and monitoring your heart rate (azumio.com).
   - **Scanadu** monitors six vitals: pulse transit time, heart rate, electrical heart activity, temperature, heart rate variability, and pulse oximetry (scanadu.com).
2. **Screen your blood yearly for your risk of getting a heart attack.**
   - **MIRISK** by Aviir offers a cardiac-risk assessment test that predicts the chances of a heart attack for a span of five years (for patients 20 years and older). The company

ran out of funding, but the science, I believe, will help other startups bring this technology to market.

GENERAL HEALTH & WELLNESS

General health apps can vary greatly in usefulness, but several worth mentioning are outlined below. In addition, several novel technologies exist that can provide you with an accurate, overall picture of individual health.

Some apps and technologies provide physician-curated information, made easy to read and understand with audiovisuals. Other companies have devised technologies for analysis of personal health components and use those parameters to create a comprehensive health plan. Fitness is another area that's exploding with opportunities in the digital health sector. Many devices can measure your physical performance, accurately report caloric expenditure, and track your progress over time.

1. **Get into a daily or weekly practice to stay healthy.**
   - **Greatist** is a website that provides health and wellness articles with great visuals (greatist.com).
   - **Inside Tracker** offers blood biomarker analysis plus interventions for nutrition, exercise, and lifestyle to optimize health (insidetracker.com).
   - **Withings Smart Body Analyzer** measures weight, body composition, heart rate, and indoor air quality (withings.com).
   - **WellnessFX** uses blood diagnostics like CBC, BUN, and other blood panels to create a specific diet and lifestyle plan (wellnessfx.com).

2. **Track your physical performance.**
   - **Basis** tracks fitness activity, heart rate, calorie expenditure, and other body demographics (mybasis.com).
   - **Nike's Fuel Band** measures movement and activity and then utilizes an online network so you can connect and share your data with your friends, allowing you to keep each other going (nike.com).
   - **Fitbit** monitors exercise, caloric intake, sleep patterns, and weight (fitbit.com).
   - **Fitbug** monitors activity and sleep; then uploads the data directly to your online account. Your digital coach analyzes your activity levels, caloric intake, and sleeps patterns, and then sets small goals for you to achieve (fitbug.com).

SEXUAL HEALTH

Sex education, sexual function, and sexual health are all making strides in the area of digital health. From getting high quality information, to getting diagnosed for sexual problems such as erectile dysfunction, and STDs, these companies are worth a look:

1. **Test for a potential STD, if you had a concerning sexual encounter.**
   - **SexualHealth** allows you to get tested for STDs, receive a diagnosis, and obtain a doctor's consult all with complete privacy for a flat rate (sexualhealth.com).
   - **Healthvana** makes the whole process of getting tested for HIV and STDs less scary and much easier. First, you can use their free Yelp-like HIV and STD testing locator to find a clinic. Next, if you go to a Healthvana-

powered clinic you get your test results back on your mobile phone in real time. And if you need treatment, it will direct you on what to do and where to go next (healthvana.com).

SEIZURE CARE

Seizure monitoring will alert patients and caregivers of an impending seizure, allowing greater safety surrounding an event.

1. **Monitor seizures and get alerted.**
   - **Neurovista's iEEG** device detects seizure signals and alerts patients when a seizure is imminent (neurovista. com).
   - **My Epilepsy Diary** records seizure event details, tracks medications, and provides alerts for missed dosages (epilepsy.com/seizuredairy).
   - **Smart Monitor** has a SmartWatch that detects seizure activity and instantly alerts caregivers (smart-monitor. com).
   - **EpDetect** detects when a patient has fallen during a seizure and alerts the caregiver (epdetect.com).

ASTHMA

Management of asthma is becoming much more streamlined, thanks to a host of new technologies. Digital asthma diaries allow patients to log attacks, potential triggers, and medication usage.

Other technologies are aimed at teaching asthmatics proper inhaler usage to ensure they're receiving the full intended dose of medication. Other devices measure wheeze rates and peak flows.

High-risk atmospheric conditions can be pinpointed with the use of apps that measure air quality and weather conditions. This data, when uploaded to a share site, creates a map of danger zones that asthmatics can avoid.

1. **Track your good and bad days.**
   - **AsthmaMD** allows you to log asthma activity, severity, triggers, location, and medications (asthmamd.org).
   - **Propeller Health** has a device that can be used with an inhaler to monitor how often it is used, so you can monitor your (or your kids) medication compliance (propellerhealth.com).
   - **AsthmaSense** tracks symptoms, triggers, and use of regularly scheduled meds, peak flow measurements, and wheeze rates (asthmasense.com).
2. **Make sure you are using your inhaler properly.**
   - Cambridge Consultants' **T-Haler** is a device that trains patients on proper inhaler usage with an interactive game (cambridgeconsultants.com/projects/t-haler-inhaler-training-device).

DEPRESSION

Mental health is an area of medicine that is benefiting from remote therapy. These technologies are allowing patients to access a therapist remotely for a counseling session via web-based videoconferencing.

Online assessment tools are available that screen for depression and other mental disorders, as well as tools that help with mood enhancement. The following devices and technologies are making positive changes to this field:

1. **Privately check out your depression risk.**
   - **Shedler QPD** is an automated mental health self-test that screens for depression and eight other psychiatric disorders (digitaldiagnostics.com).
   - **DepressionCheck** is a screening tool to assess your risk of depression, bipolar, and anxiety disorders in three minutes (find on iTunes).
2. **Track your mood.**
   - **Viary** is a digital tool for making personal development concrete, motivating, and measurable (viaryapp.com).
   - **MoodTune** offers a series of simple games that, when played regularly, can help treat depression (braintracercorp.com).
   - **SuperBetter** offers games that speed patients through the recovery process from an illness or injury (supperbetter.com).
3. **Access a therapist from home.**
   - **Breakthrough** helps you find a therapist and have therapy sessions via video chat (breakthrough.com).
   - **AbilTo** has an online platform that delivers behavioral coaching to corporate clients (for now) who've experienced life changing medical events (abilto.com).

SKIN CANCER

Cancer is a multifaceted disease process that is often on the minds of our population, as it affects all ages. The following technologies are allowing skin cancer detection and treatment to become better and more individualized:

1. **Screen your skin.**
    - **SkinVision** has the ability to scan and monitor your moles over time in order to prevent skin cancer. Take a photo of skin lesions and the app will provide recommendations on what to do next (skinvision.com).
    - **TeleSkin** educates you about potentially cancerous moles and alerts you if a mole looks abnormal. It also connects you with a dermatologist (teleskin.com).

WEIGHT LOSS

Weight loss is a goal for many people living in the US, given the obesity epidemic that has swept the nation. Apps promoting a specific diet, weight loss routine, or fitness regimen abound. We've compiled a list of the most useful ones for your benefit:

1. **Connect with others who have the same goals.**
    - **ShapeUp** has a platform so you can compete with your work colleagues (shapeup.com).
    - **SparkPeople** allows you to connect with thousands of people also looking to lose weight, which will make the process easier (sparkpeople.com).
2. **Find weight loss apps.**
    - **Loseit** provides a convenient way to follow both exercise and calories so you can make the right trade-offs between working out and eating out (loseit.com).
    - **MyDietCoach** allows users to set goals and get motivational tips to battle cravings (mydietcoachapp.com).

Digital Optimization Summary

I hope you have a much better sense of how to make your health experiences faster, better, smarter, and cheaper. So that you might think differently, I wanted to show you that there are numerous **different ways to access care and manage your health for both simple and complex conditions**. We now live in a time when we can optimize our care through digital tools and services—it just takes you to get involved.

All this change will have knock-on effects. In the coming decades, I think every health organization, hospital, and physician will have a digital strategy to engage with patients. When selecting which hospital or doctor you should go to, their digital approach might be a consideration.

One fundamental theme is that we have to become better shoppers. We need to start thinking about how to shop for better prices; get estimates for procedures and surgeries; and demand that health systems and insurers become more transparent with pricing. We should not be surprised at how much an aspirin costs!

Another fundamental theme is that we are actually the solution. When we all as patients start to help each other through patient networks, we can dramatically bring down care costs and better manage illness.

Perhaps the biggest future trend is one of personalization and care coordination. How doctors treat and communicate with patients will undergo a tremendous change. We need to seek tailored treatments and make sure that we really understand what the doctor is telling us.

Personal leadership in our own health will be the most important revolution in healthcare! We need to become better co-pilots and more engaged—digital tools are here and now is the time to do this.

Digital Optimization Highlights:

1. Proactively look for alternatives to getting the care you need through **new care options and outlets.**

2. **Mental health, wellness, nutrition, and dermatology** will become major areas for telehealth where you will be able to really optimize your care.

3. Most leading hospitals **will have a telehealth offering,** so call one up and see what they can offer you.

4. Pharmacy chains will emerge as a critical component to a**ccess healthcare, from clinics to in-store diagnostics.**

5. New health apps **are offered all the time,** so check the app stores (iTunes and Google Play) and find out if your hospital or doctor offers an app.

6. Apps for weight loss, health education, tracking, and monitoring will continue to dominate, but new apps will emerge that will allow you to access doctors and health services directly from your phone.

7. Most of us will need to **become better healthcare shoppers.** We can't just show up at a hospital or clinic without a little research on which location will offer the best value.

8. If you have a medical condition, **join a patient network.** Patients helping patients will be one of the best ways of driving down costs.

9. **Choose doctors who will embrace** new patient engagement technologies: video chats, social media platforms, tutorials, and webinars. You will be healthier in the end.

10. Don't shy away from the emerging trend of medical tourism. You may need to travel abroad to get more bang for your buck.

11. **Remember to add complementary providers** to your "health portfolio" options to optimize your care. More insurance companies are reimbursing for services like acupuncture and other alternative therapies.

CONCLUSION

We are on an exciting journey toward achieving *Health On Demand.* I hope this book has given you a clearer picture of how to prevent illness and optimize your care in this new era of medicine. I am excited to see how this profession that I love is now being remade with the tools and technologies that will make care better for all of us.

I think we will look back at this decade of medicine as a **pivotal point toward empowering consumers**. We are entering an era where medicine will move away from "one size fits all" treatments and "blanket" recommendations. Science is forging a way to deliver care specific to a person's biology and social context. Smart devices will be the engine for allowing care to become bite-sized, on demand, and 24/7. For example, insulin delivery technologies allow diabetics to increase their insulin as needed throughout the day (helpful when they want an extra piece of cheesecake). Devices like this align patient lifestyles with medical necessities.

Care will transition from inside the doctor's office to outside—it will take place in homes, on TV screens, and in cars. It will also be delivered through your clothes, through smartphones and gadgets, and in pharmacies, corporate clinics, and basically anywhere it can be done efficiently and conveniently. Moreover, the format of healthcare (such as where, when, and who provides care) is undergoing a transition similar to what has taken place in other industries.

Companies, health systems, and startups are creating a new framework to access care with a focus on the value it provides. You will need to be ready to engage with new offerings that come out of this innovation in order to make healthcare better.

But as I mentioned, many of these companies will both succeed and fail. Some failures are noted in this book in the hope that, by sharing the aspirations of entrepreneurs, you can see how big of a change might happen. I applaud the women and men who are working in both big corporations and tiny startups helping to transform the very fabric of our system.

I believe this framework will create care that is **Faster** (by engaging distributed delivery models), **Better** (by embracing pre-emptive health), **Smarter** (by demanding healthcare become more adaptive and individualized), and **Cheaper** (by fostering new networks and coordinated care efforts; and by increasing price transparency).

But for this to happen, **it will take a consumer revolution,** because unless patients engage, the opportunity to transform our system will be lost. You must demand that our system become more precise, responsive, and responsible. From this perspective, you are the critical solution to fixing healthcare. You will need to become actively involved with planning to stay well and co-piloting your care. By not relying solely on doctors, actively engaged patients will take the pressure off the bottlenecks in the current infrastructure.

To this end, the digital era of medicine will be defined as the *partnership era* where doctors, patients, and all stakeholders will be involved in keeping our country healthy!

ABOUT THE AUTHOR

Ramesh Subramani MD, MBA, MPH is the Chief Medical Officer for Analyte Health, one of the country's largest telemedicine companies which aims to break down barriers to care while improving quality and outcomes. He formerly worked in venture capital at New Leaf Ventures, did management consulting for McKinsey & Co, and was an Assistant Professor in the Department of Emergency Medicine at the Feinberg School of Medicine at Northwestern University. His career uniquely blends *medicine, technology, business, and public health*—all the while focusing on improving health systems and empowering patients. His blog is healthdisrupted.com.

He received his medical degree and residency training from Northwestern and University of Chicago, respectively. He also has degrees in engineering, business, and public health from the University of Illinois system. He received additional business training at the University of Chicago Booth School of Business.

Dr. Subramani is also passionate about helping disadvantaged young people. He started one of the largest tutoring programs for at-risk youth in Chicago and helped establish a College of Engineering for women in rural India. A number of at-risk students, he worked with, continued on to medical school. He is married and lives with his family in Chicago.

APPENDIX A
LIST OF COMPANIES AND STARTUPS
(NOT EXHAUSTIVE)

Company	Website	Details
Nutrition		
Mobile Food Coach	mobilefoodcoach.com	Food coach
Fooducate	fooducate.com	Nutrition finder
GoodGuide	goodguide.com	Food safety
Shopwell	shopwell.com	Food scanner
My Diet Coach	mydietcoach.com	Weight loss
My Food Facts	myfoodfacts.com	Food allergy
Oh My Green	ohmygreen.com	Healthy snacks
For Kids		
Pixie Scientific	pixiescientific.com	Diaper based
Trixie Tracker	trixietracker.com	Improving baby's sleep
C8 Sciences	c8sciences.com	ADHD training

Quotient	quotient-adhd.com	ADHD test
Baby Bix	babybix.com	Baby activity tracker
ScoliScore	scoliscore.com	Scoliosis
Synapdx	synapdx.com	Autism diagnostic
Teddy The Guardian	teddytheguardian.com	Monitoring vitals

Women's Health

Avva Health	avvahealth.com	Breast cancer screening
ChickRx	chickrx.com	Online magazine
Kindara	kindara.com	Pregnancy app
Baby Bump	babybumpapp.com	Pregnancy
LatchMD	latchmd.com	Lactation training
Airstrip One	airstrip.com	Fetal monitoring
Mobile Mom	mobilemom.com	Pregnancy tracker
Ovuline	ovuline.com	Fertility
Sprout Pregnancy	medart-studios.com/ sprout-pregnancy-iphone-app/	Pregnancy
Baby Center	babycenter.com	Parenting
Panorama	panoramatest.com	Pregnancy testing

Brain Health

Evoke Neuroscience	evokeneuroscience.com	Brain diagnostic
Constant Therapy	constanttherapy.com	Stroke rehab
Dakim	dakim.com	Brain training
Lumosity	lumosity.com	Brain training
AbilTo	abilto.com	Recovery
Breakthrough	breakthrough.com/ therapists	Psychologist finder
Muse	choosemuse.com	Brain training
BrainMD	brainmd.com	Brain testing

CANTABmobile	cambridgecognition.com	Memory testing
Brain Tracer	braintracercorp.com	Mood tracking
Neurotrack	neurotrack.com	Alzheimer's testing
Shedler QPD Panel	digitaldiagnostics.com	Psych screening

Better Rx

Mediguard	mediguard.org	Side effects
Med Watcher	medwatcher.org	Side effect finder
Proteus Smart Pills	proteus.com	Smart pills
Symple	sympleapp.com	Symptom tracker
Care4Today	care4today.com	Reminders
Abiogenix	abiogenix.com	Smart pill box
GlowCaps	glowcaps.com	Smart pill box
My Picture Rx	mypicturerx.com	Pill finder
Needy Meds	needymeds.org	Help paying for meds

Lower Prices

Guroo	guroo.com	Price comparison
Nerd Wallet	nerdwallet.com	Price finder
Pokidot	pokidot.com	Cost estimator
CakeHealth	cakehealth.com	Managing expense
Refermehealth	refermehealth.com	Hospital finder
Castlight Health	castlighthealth.com	Price-quality comparison
GoodRx	goodrx.com	Lower cost rx
Simplee	simplee.com	Managing expense
Cost Helper	costhelper.com	Price comparison
Health In Reach	healthinreach.com	Price comparison
HealthSparq	Healthsparq.com	Price comparison

Compass Health	compassphs.com	Concierge services

Allergy

Foods You Can	foodsyoucan.com	Food intolerance
Grain or No Grain	grainornograin.com	Gluten allergy
My Food Facts	myfoodfacts.com	Food allergy
Immune Tech	immune-tech.com	Allergy triggers
Allergy Caddy	allergycaddy.com	Food allergy

Diabetes

Omada Health	omadahealth.com	Pre-diabetes intervention
Diabetes Plus Me	diabetesplusme.com	Tracking
Diabetic Connect	diabeticconnect.com	Patient networking
AgaMatrix	agamatrix.com	Diabetes manager
CareLogger	carelogger.com	Glucose tracking
Cellnovo	cellnovo.com	Diabetes manager
DexCom	dexcom.com	Glucose monitor
Entra Health Systems	entrahealthsystems.com	Management
Glooko	glooko.com	Tracking sugar
Glucose Buddy	glucosebuddy.com	Management
Alere Connect	alere.com	Diagnostics
Medtronic	medtronic.com	Medical technology
MicroCHIPS	microchipsbiotech.com	Drug delivery
Telcare	telcare.com	Smart glucometer
WellDoc	welldoc.com	Engagement platform
Prognomix	prognomix.com	Pre-diabetes testing
Orphyx	orpyx.com	Diabetic foot monitor

Skin

SkinVision	skinvision.com	Mole analysis
UMSkinCheck	uofmhealth.org	Cancer screen
DermLink	dermlink.md	Tele derm
SkinScan	skinscan.com	Mole analysis
Spruce Health	sprucehealth.com	Tele derm
Teleskin	teleskin.org	Cancer detection
Direct Dermatology	directdermatology.com	Tele derm

Sleep

Sleepbot	mysleepbot.com	Sleep tracker
SleepCycle	sleepcycle.com	Sleep manager
Novasom	novasom.com	Home sleep study

Heart Health

iRhythm	irhythmtech.com	Monitor
AliveCor	alivecor.com	Monitor
Azumios	azumio.com	Mobile apps
XDx	allomap.com	Transplant monitor
Corventis	corventis.com	Monitor

Cancer

Allegro Diagnostics	veracyte.com	Lung cancer
Exact Sciences	exactsciences.com	Colon cancer
Pink Bra	itunes.com	Breast self exam
MolecularHealth	molecularhealth.com	Cancer detection
Oncimmune	earlycdt-lung.co.uk	Lung cancer
Cancer IQ	cancer-iq.com	Cancer care
Mira Dx	miradx.com	Cancer screen
Genomic Health	genomichealth.com	Cancer diagnostics

MDxHealth	mdxhealth.com	Cancer detection
Smart Patients	smartpatients.com	Cancer community
Myriad Genetics	myriad.com	Breast & ovarian cancer

Asthma

Propeller Health	propellerhealth.com	Smart Inhaler
AsthmaMD	asthmamd.org	Asthma control
AsthmaSense	asthmasense.com	Reminders app
Cohero Health	coherohealth.com	Smart peak flow
My Spiroo	myspiroo.com	Smart peak flow

Seizures

Epdetect	epdetect.com	Seizure detection
My Epilepsy Diary	epilepsy.com/get-help/my-epilepsy-diary	Seizure management
Smart Watch	smart-monitor.com	Fall monitor
NeuroVista	neurovista.com	Seizure detection
Neuropace	neuropace.com	Treatment

Personalized Medicine

23andMe	23andme.com	DNA service
Pathway Genomics	pathway.com	Wellness oriented
Invitae	invitae.com	Affordable testing
GeneDx	genedx.com	Rare disorders
InsideTracker	insidetracker.com	Fitness oriented
DNA Direct	dnadirect.com	Targets hospitals
VectraDA	vectrada.com	Rheumatoid arthritis
Cell Tex	celltexbank.com	Stem cell banking
Editas Medicine	editasmedicine.com	Gene editing
GeneomeDx	genomedx.com	Prostate cancer

Patient Tools

Symcat	symcat.com	Symptom triage
WellApps	wellapps.com	Symptom tracker
Senstore	senstore.com	Virtual nurse
Crohnology	crohnology.com	Crohn's tracking
Healthvana	healthvana.com	Test result enhancement
DocSpot	docspot.com	Doctor finder
Limeade	limeade.com	Employee engagement
Give Forward	giveforward.com	Medical fundraiser
Real Self	realself.com	Cosmetic procedure finder

Communication Tools

Visible Health Connect	visiblehealth.com	Patient engagement
HealthVoice App	healthvoiceapp.com	Doctors notes
MediBabble	medibabble.com	Medical translator
DrawMD	drawmd.com	Medical visuals
Emmi Solutions	emmisolutions.com	Informed consent
Agile Diagnostics	agilemd.com	Medical education
HealthCrowd	healthcrowd.com	Messaging platform
Docphin	docphin.com	Medical journals
Orca health	orcahealth.com	Visual communication

Care Collaboration

CaringBridge	caringbridge.org	Health journal
PatientsLikeMe	patientslikeme.com	Patient to patient network

Fibroblast	fibroblast.com	Follow-up appointment
QuantiaMD	quantiamd.com	Doctor to doctor
Care Giver	caregiver.org	Caregiving
Sermo	sermo.com	Doctor to doctor
My Health Teams	myhealthteams.com	Chronic conditions community

Diagnostics

WellnessFX	wellnessfx.com	Health diagnostics
Home Access	homeaccess.com	Home testing
NanoRETE	nanorete.com	TB screening
OraSure	orasure.com	HIV testing
T2 Biosystems	t2biosystems.com	Fungal testing
Theranos	theranos.com	Testing at Walgreens
CardioDx	cardiodx.com	Genomic diagnostics
Boston Heart	bostonheartdiagnostics.com	Heart health management

Second Opinion

MetaMed	metamed.com	Second opinion
iRapidConsultant	irapidconsult.com	Spine second opinion
Grand Rounds	grandroundshealth.com	Second opinion

Faster Access

Solohealth	solohealth.com	Kiosk
ZocDoc	zocdoc.com	Doctor finder
HealthTap.com	healthtap.com	Q&A
DoctorOnDemand	doctorondemand.com	Video consultation
MDAligne	mdaligne.com	Telehealth

Zipnosis	zipnosis.com	Telehealth
Teladoc	teladoc.com	Telehealth
American Well	americanwell.com	Telehealth
Analyte	analytehealth.com	Online diagnostics
Consultadoc	consultadoc.co.uk	Telehealth
EyeNetra	eyenetra.com	Eye testing
MDLive	mdlive.com	Telehealth
NoviMedicine	novimedicine.com	Virtual office
Premise health	premisehealth.com	Onsite healthcare
First Stop Health	fshealth.com	Telehealth

Patient Education

Share Care	sharecare.com	Wellness platform
HealthGuru	healthguru.com	Health videos
Found Health	foundhealth.com	Treatment options
Cleveland Clinic	my.clevelandclinic.org	Health portal
Health Central	healthcentral.com	Health and wellness
Wellsphere	wellsphere.com	Online health
Healthination	healthination.com	Video based
Healthline	healthline.com	Online health
HealthMap	healthmap.org	Outbreak alert
Healthism	healthism.com	Virtual care
Mayo Clinic	mayoclinic.org	Web portal
MedHelp	medhelp.org	Community wellness
Alliance Healthcare	alliancehealthcare.com	Patient network
Inner Body	innerbody.com	Virtual anatomy
Greatist	greatist.com	Virtual wellness
Health	health.com	Virtual wellness
Institute of Med	iom.edu	Web portal
Intelihealth	intelihealth.com	Harvard content

Longwood Herbal	longwoodherbal.org	Herbal information

Activity Monitoring/ Social Health

Lose it!	loseit.com	Weight loss
SparkPeople	sparkpeople.com	Weight loss
ShapeUp	shapeup.com	Social health
Basis	mybasis.com	Tracker
Fitbit	fitbit.com	Tracker
Fitbug	fitbug.com	Tracker
NikeFuel	nike.com/NikeFuel	Tracker
Up by Jawbone	jawbone.com/up	Tracker
Voxiva	voxiva.com	Text messaging
Scanadu	scanadu.com	Tracking device
MC10	mc10inc.com	Band-Aid like monitor
SuperBetter	superbetter.com	Gaming for wellness
Misfit	misfit.com	Tracker
Rally Health	rallyhealth.com	Health manager

Devices

Withings	withings.com	Home devices
Cellscope	cellscope.com	Ear infections
Organovo	organovo.com	Bioprinting
Biorasis	bio-orasis.com	Implantable monitor

Medical Tourism

MedRetreat	medretreat.com	Medical travel
MedToGo	medtogo.com	Medical referral
Planet Hospital	planethospital.com	Medical travel

Alternative Care

Buddhify	buddhify.com	Meditation
Do Yoga With Me	doyogawithme.com	Online yoga
MindBody Online	mindbodyonline.com	Wellness finder
MyHeadspace	headspace.com	Meditation

Other

Fount.in	Fount.in	Infection outbreak

APPENDIX B
ADDITIONAL RESOURCES

Health Incubators

Healthbox – healthbox.com

Rock Health – rockhealth.com

Blueprint Health – blueprinthealth.org

StartX Med – startx.stanford.edu

Wearable World Labs – wearableworldlabs.com

Launchpad Digital Health – launchpdh.com

Health News Sources

Medcitynews.com

Mobihealthnews.com

Fiercehealthcare.com

Thejournalofmhealth.com

Healthdisrupted.com

iMedicalapps.com

genomeweb.com

Healthcare Pricing Information

Costhelper.com

Healthcarebluebook.com

Guroo.com

Healthinreach.com

ENDNOTES

1   Based on article written by Sarah Mann in the Association of American Medical Colleges: "Addressing the Physician Shortage Under Reform." April 2011.

2   www.thecentenarian.co.uk/how-many-people-live-to-hundred-across-the-globe.html

3   Based on article written by Dr. Michael Roizen in The Huffington Post: "Why Health Coaching Will Create American Jobs." December 10, 2010.

4   http://www.theatlantic.com/health/archive/2012/09/the-289-billion-cost-of-medication-noncompliance-and-what-to-do-about-it/262222/

5   CIN: Computers, Informatics, Nursing: October 2013 – Volume 31 – Issue 10 - p 469-476

6   http://www.telenor.com/news-and-media/press-releases/2012/new-study-the-world-is-ready-for-mobile-healthcare/

7   http://www.sca-aware.org/for-the-media

8   http://www.abiresearch.com/press/wearable-sports-and-fitness-devices-will-hit-90-mi

9   MIT Tech Review magazine article by Emily Singer: "Faster Tools to Scrutinize the Genome." February 23, 2010.

10   http://www.ncbi.nlm.nih.gov/pmc/articles/PMC3614010/

11   http://www.iata.org/pressroom/pr/Pages/2013-12-30-01.
aspx

12   http://www.pewinternet.org/Press-Releases/2013/Health-
Online-2013.aspx

13   www.depressionperception.com

14   http://www.adaa.org/about-adaa/press-room/facts-
statistics

15   http://www.mentalhealthconnection.org/pdfs/brc-final-
report-full.pdf

16   http://www.adaa.org/about-adaa/press-room/facts-
statistics; http://www.livescience.com/5997-depressed-
americans-treatment.html

17   Based on article written by Dr. Michael Flaum for the
Department of Human Services: "Telemental Health as a
solution to the widening gap between supply and demand
for mental health services."

18   Ibid.

19   Based on multiple sources – presenteeism and absenteeism
ranging from $40 to $100 billion plus.

20   Based on article written by Beth Kowitt in CNN Money:
"Starbucks CEO: 'We spend more on health care than
coffee.'" June 7, 2010.

21   http://www.washingtonpost.com/wp-dyn/articles/
A15828-2005Feb10.html

22   Based on transcripts from CNN "Escape Fire"; The Fight To
Save American Healthcare.

23   From University of New Hampshire Institute of Medicine:
      "Study On Making Sense Of Geographic Variation In Health
      Care Spending." May 2013.

24   http://budgeting.thenest.com/average-price-hospital-bills-
      pregnancy-24229.html

25   http://lifegenetics.net/weight-loss-dna-diet/

26   http://www.acpm.org/?MedAdhereTTProviders

27   http://www.webmd.com/hypertension-high-blood-
      pressure/news/20010611/acupuncture-can-lower-high-
      blood-pressure

28   Based on McKinsey and Company: "Healthy, wealthy and
      (maybe) wise: The emerging trillion-dollar market for health
      and wellness." May 2012.

29   Per consulting firm Deloitte and Touché Medical Tourism:
      "Update and implications."

30   Based on Dr. Foster's UK website approximate wait time
      is 57 days for surgery. "The Guardian newspaper reports
      6-month wait time for bypass surgery." February 2005.

31   http://online.wsj.com/article/SB10001424127887323393804
      578555741780608174.html